TIMED READING

25 Two-Part Lessons
with Questions for
Building Reading Speed and Comprehension

BOOK TWO

Edward Spargo

JAMESTOWN PUBLISHERS

a division of NTC/CONTEMPORARY PUBLISHING GROUP
Lincolnwood, Illinois USA

Timed Readings Plus, Book Two, Level E

Selection text adapted from Compton's Encyclopedia.
Used with permission of Compton's Learning Company.

ISBN: 0-89061-904-2

Published by Jamestown Publishers,
a division of NTC/Contemporary Publishing Group, Inc.,
4255 West Touhy Avenue,
Lincolnwood, Illinois, 60646 U.S.A.

890 ML 098765432

CONTENTS

TO THE INSTRUCTOR

Overview

Timed Readings Plus is designed to develop both reading speed and comprehension. A timed selection in each lesson focuses on improving reading rate. A nontimed selection—the "plus" selection—follows the timed selection. The nontimed selection concentrates on building mastery in critical areas of comprehension.

The 10 books in the series span reading levels 4–13, with one book at each level. Readability of the selections was assessed by using the Fry Readability Scale. Each book contains 25 lessons; each lesson is divided into Parts A and B.

Part A includes the timed selection followed by 10 multiple-choice questions: 5 fact questions and 5 thought questions. The timed selection is 400 words long and contains subject matter that is factual, nonfiction, and textbook-like. Because everyone—regardless of level—reads a 400-word passage, the steps for the timed selection can be concurrent for everyone.

Part B includes the nontimed selection, which is more narrative than the timed selection. The length of the selection varies depending on the subject matter, which relates to the content of the timed selection. The nontimed selection is followed by five comprehension questions that address the following major comprehension skills: recognizing words in context, distinguishing fact from opinion, keeping events in order, making correct inferences, and understanding main ideas.

Getting Started

Begin by assigning students to a level. A student should start with a book that is one level below his or her current reading level. If a student's reading level is not known, a suitable starting point would be one or two levels below the student's present grade in school.

Teaching a Lesson: Part A

Work in each lesson begins with the timed selection in Part A. If you wish to have all the students in the class read a selection at the same time, you can coordinate the timing using the following method. Give students the signal to preview. Allow 15 seconds for this. Have students begin reading the selection at the same time. After one minute has passed, write on the chalkboard the time that has elapsed. Update the time at 10-second intervals (1:00, 1:10, 1:20, etc.). Tell students to copy down the last time shown on the chalkboard when they finish reading. They should then record this reading time in the space designated after the selection.

If students keep track of their own reading times, have them write the times at which they start and finish reading on a separate piece of paper and then figure and record their reading time as above.

Students should now answer the ten questions that follow the Part A selection. Responses are recorded by putting an X in the box next to the student's choice of answer. Correct responses to eight or more questions indicates satisfactory comprehension and recall.

Teaching a Lesson: Part B

When students have finished Part A, they can move on to read the Part B selection. Although brief, these selections deliver all the content needed to attack the range of comprehension questions that follow.

Students next answer the comprehension questions that follow the Part B selection. Directions for answering the questions are provided with each question. Correct responses require deliberation and discrimination.

Correcting and Scoring Answers

Using the Answer Key at the back of the book, students self-score their responses to the questions in Parts A and B. Incorrect answers should be circled and the correct answers should be marked. The number of correct answers for Part A and for Part B and the total correct answers should be tallied on the final page of the lesson.

Using the Graphs

Reading times are plotted on the Reading Rate graph at the back of the book. The legend on the graph automatically converts reading times to words-per-minute rates. Comprehension totals are plotted on the Comprehension Scores graph. Plotting automatically converts the raw scores to a comprehension percentage based on four points per correct answer.

Diagnosis and Evaluation

The Comprehension Skills Profile graph at the back of the book tracks student responses to the Part B comprehension questions. For each incorrect response, students should mark an X in the corresponding box on the graph. A column of Xs rising above other columns indicates a specific comprehension weakness. Using the profile, you can assess trends in student performance and suggest remedial work if necessary.

A student who has reached a peak in reading speed (with satisfactory comprehension) is ready to advance to the next book in the series. Before moving on to the next book, students should be encouraged to maintain their speed and comprehension on a number of lessons in order to consolidate their achievement.

How to Use This Book

Getting Started

Study Part A: Reading Faster and Better. Read and learn the steps to follow and the techniques to use to help you read more quickly and more efficiently.

Study Part B: Mastering Reading Comprehension. Learn what the five categories of comprehension are all about. Knowing what kind of comprehension response is expected from you and how to achieve that response will help you better comprehend all you read.

Working a Lesson

Find the Starting Lesson. Locate the timed selection in Part A of the lesson that you are going to read. Wait for your instructor's signal to preview the selection. Your instructor will allow you 15 seconds for previewing.

Read the Part A Selection. When your instructor gives you the signal, begin reading. Read at a faster-than-normal speed. Read carefully so that you will be able to answer questions about what you have read.

Record Your Reading Time. When you finish reading, look at the blackboard and note your reading time. Write this time at the bottom of the page on the line labeled Reading Time.

Answer the Part A Questions. Answer the 10 questions that follow the selection. There are 5 fact questions and 5 thought questions. Choose the best answer to each question and put an X in that box.

Read the Part B Selection. This passage is less textbook-like and more story-like than the timed selection. Read well enough so that you can answer the questions that follow.

Answer the Part B Questions. These questions are different from traditional multiple-choice questions. In answering these questions, you must make three choices for each question. Instructions for answering each category of question are given. There are 15 responses for you to record.

Correct Your Answers. Use the Answer Key at the back of the book. For the Part A questions, circle any wrong answer and put an X in the box you should have marked. For the Part B questions, circle any wrong answer and write the correct letter or number next to it.

Scoring Your Work

Total Your Correct Answers. Count your correct answers for Part A and for Part B. Record those numbers on the appropriate lines at the end of the lesson. Then add the two scores to determine your total correct answers. Record that number on the appropriate line.

Plotting Your Progress

Plot Your Reading Time. Refer to the Reading Rate graph on page 116. On the vertical line that represents your lesson, put an X at the point where it intersects your reading time, shown along the left-hand side. The right-hand side of the graph will reveal your words-per-minute reading speed. Your instructor will review this graph from time to time to evaluate your progress.

Plot Your Comprehension Scores. Record your comprehension scores on the graph on page 117. On the vertical line that represents your lesson, put an X at the point where it intersects your total correct answers, shown along the left-hand side. The right-hand side of the graph will reveal your comprehension percentage. Your instructor will want to review this graph, too. Your achievement, as shown on both graphs, will determine your readiness to move on to higher and more challenging levels.

Plot Your Comprehension Skills. You will find the Comprehension Skills Profile on page 118. It is used to record your wrong answers only for the Part B questions. The five categories of questions are listed along the bottom. There are five columns of boxes, one column for each question. For every wrong answer, put an X in a box for that question. Your instructor will use this graph to detect any comprehension problems you may be experiencing.

PART A: READING FASTER AND BETTER

Step 1: Preview

When you read, do you start in with the first word, or do you look over the whole selection for a moment? Good readers preview the selection first. This helps make them good—and fast—readers. Here are the steps to follow when previewing the timed selection in Part A of each unit.

1. Read the Title. Titles are designed not only to announce the subject, but also to make the reader think. What can you learn from the title? What thoughts does it bring to mind? What do you already know about this subject?

2. Read the First Sentence. Read the first two sentences if they are short. The opening sentence is the writer's opportunity to greet the reader. Some writers announce what they hope to tell you in the selection. Some writers tell you why they are writing. Other writers just try to get your attention.

3. Read the Last Sentence. Read the final two sentences if they are short. The closing sentence is the writer's last chance to talk to you. Some writers repeat the main idea once more. Some writers draw a conclusion—this is what they have been leading up to. Other writers summarize their thoughts; they tie all the facts together.

4. Scan the Selection. Glance through the selection quickly to see what else you can pick up. Look for anything that can help you read the selection. Are there names, dates, or numbers? If so, you may have to read more slowly. Is the selection informative—containing a lot of facts, or is it conversational—an informal discussion with the reader?

Step 2: Read for Meaning

When you read, do you just see words? Are you so occupied reading words that you sometimes fail to get the meaning? Good readers see beyond the words—they seek the meaning. This makes them faster readers.

1. Build Concentration. You cannot read with understanding if you are not concentrating. When you discover that your thoughts are straying, correct the situation right away. Avoid distractions and distracting situations. Keep the preview information in mind. This will help focus your attention on the selection.

2. Read in Thought Groups. A reader should strive to see words in meaningful combinations. If you see only a word at a time (called word-by-word reading), your comprehension suffers along with your speed.

3. Question the Writer. To sustain the pace you have set for yourself, and to maintain a high level of concentration and comprehension, question the writer as you read. Ask yourself such questions as, "What does this mean? How can I use this information?"

Step 3: Grasp Paragraph Sense

The paragraph is the basic unit of meaning. If you can discover quickly and understand the main point of each paragraph, you can comprehend the writer's message. Good readers know how to find the main ideas quickly. This helps make them faster readers.

1. Find the Topic Sentence. The topic sentence, which contains the main idea, is often the first sentence of a paragraph. It is followed by sentences that support, develop, or explain the main idea. Sometimes a topic sentence comes at the end of a paragraph. When it does, the supporting details come first, building the base for the topic sentence. Some paragraphs do not have a topic sentence; all of the sentences combine to create a meaningful idea.

2. Understand Paragraph Structure. Every well-written paragraph has a purpose. The purpose may be to inform, define, explain, illustrate, and so on. The purpose should always relate to the main idea and expand on it. As you read each paragraph, see how the body of the paragraph is used to tell you more about the main idea.

Step 4: Organize Facts

When you read, do you tend to see a lot of facts without any apparent connection or relationship? Understanding how the facts all fit together to deliver the writer's message is, after all, the reason for reading. Good readers organize facts as they read. This helps them read rapidly and well.

1. Discover the Writer's Plan. Every writer has a plan or outline to follow. If you can discover the writer's method of organization, you have a key to understanding the message. Sometimes the writer gives you obvious signals. The statement, "There are three reasons . . .," should prompt you to look for a listing of the three items. Other less obvious signal words such as *moreover, otherwise,* and *consequently* tell you the direction the writer is taking in delivering a message.

2. Relate as You Read. As you read the selection, keep the information learned during the preview in mind. See how the writer is attempting to piece together a meaningful message. As you discover the relationship among the ideas, the message comes through quickly and clearly.

PART B: MASTERING READING COMPREHENSION

Recognizing Words in Context

Always check to see if the words around a new word—its context—can give you some clue to its meaning. A word generally appears in a context related to its meaning. If the words *soil* and *seeds* appear in an article about gardens, for example, you can assume they are related to the topic of gardens.

Suppose you are unsure of the meaning of the word *expired* in the following paragraph:

> Vera wanted to take a book out, but her library card had expired.
> She had to borrow mine because she didn't have time to renew hers.

You could begin to figure out the meaning of *expired* by asking yourself, "What could have happened to Vera's library card that would make her have to borrow someone else's card?" You might realize that if she had to renew her card, it must have come to an end or run out. This would lead you to conclude that the word *expired* must mean to come to an end or run out. You would be right. The context suggested the meaning to you.

Context can also affect the meaning of a word you know. The word *key,* for instance, has many meanings. There are musical keys, door keys, and keys to solving a mystery. The context in which *key* occurs will tell you which meaning is right.

Sometimes a hard word will be explained by the words that immediately follow it. The word *grave* in the following sentence might give you trouble:

> He looked grave; there wasn't a trace of a smile on his lips.

You can figure out that the second part of the sentence explains the word *grave:* "wasn't a trace of a smile" indicates a serious look, so *grave* must mean serious.

The subject of a sentence and your knowledge about that subject might also help you determine the meaning of an unknown word. Try to decide the meaning of the word *revive* in the following sentence:

> Sunshine and water will revive those drooping plants.

The sentence is about giving plants light and water. You may know that plants need light and water to be healthy. If you know that drooping plants are not healthy, you can figure out that *revive* means to bring back to health.

Distinguishing Fact from Opinion

Every day you are called upon to sort out fact and opinion. When a friend says she saw Mel Gibson's greatest movie last night, she is giving you her opinion. When she says she saw Mel Gibson's latest movie, she may be stating a fact. The fact can be proved—you can check to confirm or verify that the movie is indeed Mel Gibson's most recent film. The opinion can be disputed—ask around and others may not agree about the film's unqualified greatness. Because much of what you read and hear contains both facts and opinions, you need to be able to tell them apart. You need the skill of distinguishing fact from opinion.

Facts are statements that can be proved true. The proof must be objective and verifiable. You must be able to check for yourself to confirm a fact.

Look at the following facts. Notice that they can be checked for accuracy and confirmed. Suggested sources for verification appear in parentheses.

- In 1998 Bill Clinton was president of the United States. (Consult newspapers, news broadcasts, election results, etc.)

- Earth revolves around the sun. (Look it up in encyclopedias or astrological journals; ask knowledgeable people.)

- Dogs walk on four legs. (See for yourself.)

Opinions are statements that cannot be proved true. There is no objective evidence you can consult to check the truthfulness of an opinion. Unlike facts, opinions express personal beliefs or judgments. Opinions reveal how someone feels about a subject, not the facts about that subject. You might agree or disagree with someone's opinion, but you cannot prove it right or wrong.

Look at the following opinions. Reasons for classification as opinions appear in parentheses.

- Bill Clinton was born to be a president. (You cannot prove this by referring to birth records. There is no evidence to support this belief.)

- Intelligent life exists on other planets in our solar system. (There is no proof of this. It may be proved true some day, but for now it is just an educated guess—not a fact.)

- Dog is man's best friend. (This is not a fact; your best friend might not be a dog.)

As you read, be aware that facts and opinions are frequently mixed together. The following passage contains both facts and opinions:

> The new 2000 Cruising Yacht offers lots of real-life interior room. It features a luxurious aft cabin, not some dim "cave." The galley

comes equipped with a full-size refrigerator and freezer. And this spacious galley has room to spare. The heads (there are two) have separate showers. The fit and finish are beyond equal and the performance is responsive and outstanding.

Did you detect that the third and fifth sentences state facts and that the rest of the sentences express opinions? Both facts and opinions are useful to you as a reader. But to evaluate what you read and to read intelligently, you need to know the difference between them.

Keeping Events in Order

Writers organize details in a pattern. They present information in a certain order. Recognizing how writers organize—and understanding that organization—can help you improve your comprehension.

When details are arranged in the precise order in which they occurred, a writer is using a chronological (or time) pattern. A writer may, however, change this order. The story may "flash back" to past events that affected the present. The story may "flash forward" to show the results of present events. The writer may move back and forth between past, present, and future to help you see the importance of events.

Making Correct Inferences

Much of what you read suggests more than it says. Writers do not always state outright what they want you to know. Frequently, they omit information that underlies the statements they make. They may assume that you already know it. They may want you to make the effort to figure out the implied information. To get the most out of what you read, you must come to an understanding about unstated information. You can do this through inference. From what is stated, you make inferences about what is not.

You make many inferences every day. Imagine, for example, that you are visiting a friend's house for the first time. You see a bag of dog food. You infer (make an inference) that the family has a dog. On another day you overhear a conversation. You catch the names of two actors and the words *scene, dialogue,* and *directing.* You infer that the people are discussing a movie or play.

In these situations and others like them, you infer unstated information from what you observe or read. Readers who cannot make inferences cannot see beyond the obvious. For the careful reader, facts are just the beginning. Facts stimulate your mind to think beyond them—to make an inference about what is meant but not stated.

The following passage is about Charles Dickens. As you read it, see how many inferences you can make.

Charles Dickens visited the United States in 1867. Wherever he went, the reception was the same. The night before, crowds arrived and lined up before the door. By morning the streets were campgrounds, with men, women, and children sitting or sleeping on blankets. Hustlers got ten times the price of a ticket. Once inside, audiences were surprised to hear their favorite Dickens characters speak with an English accent. After 76 readings Dickens boarded a ship for England. When his fellow passengers asked him to read, he said he'd rather be put in irons!

Did you notice that many inferences may be drawn from the passage? Dickens attracted huge crowds. From that fact you can infer that he was popular. His English accent surprised audiences. You can infer that many people didn't know he was English. Hustlers got high prices for tickets. This suggests that "scalping" tickets is not new. Dickens refused to read on the ship. You can infer that he was exhausted and tired of reading aloud to audiences. Those are some obvious inferences that can be made from the passage. More subtle ones can also be made; however, if you see the obvious ones, you understand how inferences are made.

Be careful about the inferences you make. One set of facts may suggest several inferences. Not all of them will be correct; some will be faulty inferences. The correct inference is supported by enough evidence to make it more likely than other inferences.

Understanding Main Ideas

The main idea tells who or what is the subject of the paragraph or passage. The main idea is the most important idea, the idea that provides purpose and direction. The rest of the paragraph or passage explains, develops, or supports the main idea. Without a main idea, there would be only a collection of unconnected thoughts. It would be like a handle and a bowl without the "idea cup," or bread and meat without the "idea sandwich."

In the following passage, the main idea is printed in italics. As you read, observe how the other sentences develop or explain the main idea.

> *Typhoon Chris hit with full fury today on the central coast of Japan.* Heavy rain from the storm flooded the area. High waves carried many homes into the sea. People now fear that the heavy rains will cause mudslides in the central part of the country. The number of people killed by the storm may climb past the 200 mark by Saturday.

In this paragraph, the main idea statement appears first. It is followed by sentences that explain, support, or give details. Sometimes the main idea appears at the end of a paragraph. Writers often construct that type of paragraph when their purpose is to persuade or convince. Readers may be more open to a new idea if the reasons for it are presented first. As you read the following paragraph, think about the overall impact of the supporting ideas. Their purpose is to convince the reader that the main idea in the last sentence should be accepted.

> Last week there was a head-on collision at Huntington and Canton streets. Just a month ago a pedestrian was struck there. Fortunately, she was only slightly injured. In the past year there have been more accidents there than at any other corner in the city. In fact, nearly 10 percent of all city accidents occur there. This intersection is dangerous, and a traffic signal should be installed there before a life is lost.

The details in the paragraph progress from least important to most important. They achieve their full effect in the main idea statement at the end.

In many cases, the main idea is not expressed in a single sentence. The reader is called upon to interpret all of the ideas expressed and decide upon a main idea. Read the following paragraph:

> The American author Jack London was once a pupil at the Cole Grammar School in Oakland, California. Each morning the class sang a song. When the teacher noticed that Jack wouldn't sing, she sent him to the principal. He returned to class with a note. It said that he could be excused from singing if he would write an essay every morning.

In this paragraph, the reader has to interpret the individual ideas and decide on a main idea. This main idea seems reasonable: Jack London's career as a writer began with a "punishment" in grammar school.

Understanding the concept of the main idea and knowing how to find it is important. Transferring that understanding to your reading and study is also important.

The Dragonfly

Among the most beautiful and useful of all insects is the dragonfly. It has thin silvery wings. Its body may be steel blue, purple, green, or copper. The dragonfly eats mosquitoes, flies, and other insects harmful to people. It lives on or near the water. The dragonfly is a quick, darting insect that flies swiftly from place to place. Sometimes it changes its direction so quickly in midflight that its sudden movement is hard to follow with the eye. It can also hover over a lake or stream as it looks for food.

The dragonfly's wings are from 2 to 5 inches (5 to 12 centimeters) long. Its body is about 3 inches (8 centimeters) long. Its six legs are far forward and close together. The dragonfly can curve its legs to form a basket. It uses this basket to scoop insects from the air. Then it puts them into its jaws. These jaws have strong teeth. Two great eyes cover most of its head. Each eye has from 20,000 to 25,000 tiny eyes joined together. With these big eyes the dragonfly can see its prey easily.

There are two large groups of these insects—the dragonflies themselves and the damselflies. Dragonflies dart with the speed of an express train. Some can fly sixty miles (97 kilometers) an hour. Their two rear wings are larger than the front pair. They are held outspread when the dragonfly lands. The damselfly is more slender. It flies more slowly and lazily. Its wings are the same size. When the damselfly rests, its wings come together over its back, like a butterfly's.

The dragonfly begins life as a water insect. Then it is called a nymph. The female lays her eggs in the water. As she flies over the pond again and again, she dips underwater to wash off the eggs. Some species lay their eggs in long strings on water plants. Such a string may have 100,000 eggs.

The damselfly cuts a slit in the stems of water plants. Then she puts her eggs in the opening. Sometimes the damselfly goes underwater and walks about looking for a good cradle for the eggs.

The nymphs hatch out of the eggs in one to four weeks. In winter they sleep in the streambed. The following spring, the life cycle begins once again. When they reach the adult stage, dragonflies live for only a few months.

Reading Time _____

Recalling Facts

1. Dragonflies eat insects that
   - ❏ a. are harmful to people.
   - ❏ b. are useful to people.
   - ❏ c. do not bother people.

2. Dragonfly wings are
   - ❏ a. large and bulky.
   - ❏ b. thin and silvery.
   - ❏ c. wide and silky.

3. A dragonfly's head is mostly
   - ❏ a. eyes.
   - ❏ b. jaws.
   - ❏ c. wings.

4. Damselflies fly
   - ❏ a. like butterflies.
   - ❏ b. faster than dragonflies.
   - ❏ c. more slowly than dragonflies.

5. As adults, dragonflies live
   - ❏ a. in the stems of water plants.
   - ❏ b. mostly underwater.
   - ❏ c. only a few months.

Understanding Ideas

6. You can conclude from the article that dragonfly wings are
   - ❏ a. decorative.
   - ❏ b. efficient.
   - ❏ c. protective.

7. A dragonfly might need to lay 100,000 eggs because
   - ❏ a. dragonfly eggs are small.
   - ❏ b. most of the eggs do not survive.
   - ❏ c. the world needs more dragonflies.

8. One thing dragonflies and damselflies have in common is
   - ❏ a. the size of their wings.
   - ❏ b. their flying speed.
   - ❏ c. the place where they live.

9. According to the article, people should think of the dragonfly as
   - ❏ a. an enemy.
   - ❏ b. a friend.
   - ❏ c. a pest.

10. In winter the nymphs sleep in the streambed, which suggests that they are
    - ❏ a. delicate.
    - ❏ b. hardy.
    - ❏ c. lost.

Long ago, on a bright, warm summer day, a beautiful purple dragonfly and a small green frog were resting in the tall grass on the bank of a slow-moving river.

"You know, I'm very special," bragged the beautiful dragonfly.

"How are you special?" asked the frog lazily.

"I've lived in the water and out of it," declared the dragonfly. "As a nymph, I lived underwater and breathed through gills. I swam around and ate other water insects. Then I turned into an adult and came out to live on land."

"Well, I don't think that's so special," said the frog. "I've had the same sort of life. As a tadpole, I lived underwater and breathed through gills. I swam around and ate plants. Then I turned into an adult and came out to live on land."

"But I can fly!" exclaimed the dragonfly. "I can fly far and fast. I dart quickly here and there and scoop insects out of the air for a meal. What can you do that's so special?"

"I can dart my long, sticky tongue out quickly and scoop insects out of the air for a meal," replied the frog. Whap! And that's just what the frog did.

1. **Recognizing Words in Context**

   Find the word *dart* in the passage. One definition below is a *synonym* for that word; it means the same or almost the same thing. One definition is an *antonym;* it has the opposite or nearly opposite meaning. The other has a completely different meaning. Label the definitions S for *synonym,* A for *antonym,* and D for *different.*

   _____ a. arrow

   _____ b. dash

   _____ c. plod

2. **Distinguishing Fact from Opinion**

   Two of the statements below present *facts,* which can be proved correct. The other statement is an *opinion,* which expresses someone's thoughts or beliefs. Label the statements F for *fact* and O for *opinion.*

   _____ a. "As a nymph, I lived underwater and breathed through gills."

   _____ b. "Well, I don't think that's so special," said the frog.

   _____ c. "I can dart quickly here and there and scoop insects out of the air for a meal."

3. Keeping Events in Order

Two of the statements below describe events that happened at the same time. The other statement describes an event that happened before or after those events. Label them S for *same time*, B for *before*, and A for *after*.

_____ a. The dragonfly nymph lived underwater.

_____ b. The dragonfly flew through the air.

_____ c. The dragonfly nymph breathed through gills.

4. Making Correct Inferences

Two of the statements below are correct *inferences*, or reasonable guesses. They are based on information in the passage. The other statement is an incorrect, or faulty, inference. Label the statements C for *correct* inference and F for *faulty* inference.

_____ a. The frog was upset because it couldn't fly.

_____ b. The frog ate the dragonfly.

_____ c. Both frogs and dragonflies go through many changes before they become adults.

5. Understanding Main Ideas

One of the statements below expresses the main idea of the passage. One statement is too general, or too broad. The other explains only part of the passage; it is too narrow. Label the statements M for *main idea*, B for *too broad*, and N for *too narrow*.

_____ a. Both dragonflies and frogs begin their lives underwater, live on land as adults, and eat insects.

_____ b. Young dragonflies are called nymphs.

_____ c. Metamorphosis is a process by which an animal undergoes great changes in body structure in becoming an adult.

Correct Answers, Part A _____

Correct Answers, Part B _____

Total Correct Answers _____

Is It Alive?

Living things include plants and animals. They live on the land and in the lakes, rivers, and seas. Billions of tiny microbes live in both water and soil. These many plants, animals, and microbes are very different from one another. Yet all of them have one thing in common: they are alive. What does being "alive" mean? Perhaps there are tests for living, such as eating and moving. But will all the tests apply to every living thing? Does everything that is alive move and eat?

A good way to find answers to questions about life is to study some common animals, such as dogs. They move even when asleep. They also respond to their surroundings. They dodge when people try to catch them but come when they are offered food.

Dogs use food in many ways. Young ones use it to grow. When they are older, they use it to repair worn-out parts of their bodies. Dogs get energy from food. They use energy when they run, play, eat, and even while they sleep. Finally, dogs mate and reproduce, which means that they have young ones. Will these same tests apply to plants as well?

Plants do not try to move when they are touched (except for the "sensitive" plants). But they do change position as they grow. A tree moves its branches and leaves to get sunlight. If a plant starts to grow in a dark spot, it will turn its stem to reach the light. Plants also turn their roots to reach water and minerals in the soil.

Plants therefore move in ways that are useful to them, just as animals do. This is the kind of motion that identifies living things. By contrast, nonliving things move only if an outside force compels them to.

Although plants do not eat, they do secure food and use it. Most plants take water, nitrogen, and minerals from the soil and a gas called carbon dioxide from the air. They use these materials to make the foods they need for growth and energy. They also make some foods, which can be stored for later use.

Plants reproduce in a number of ways. Many kinds have seeds that grow into new plants. Others grow from roots, pieces of stem, or bulbs. Some kinds even reproduce by means of leaves that grow into new plants when they fall on moist, rich ground.

Reading Time _____

Recalling Facts

1. If a plant starts to grow in a dark spot, it will
   - ❏ a. die.
   - ❏ b. turn its stem to reach the light.
   - ❏ c. grow deeper roots.

2. Nonliving things
   - ❏ a. try to move when they are touched.
   - ❏ b. move only when an outside force compels them to.
   - ❏ c. move to get food.

3. Dogs use food
   - ❏ a. for growth and energy.
   - ❏ b. to make nitrogen.
   - ❏ c. only when forced.

4. Plants and animals move
   - ❏ a. to get sunlight.
   - ❏ b. in ways that are useful to them.
   - ❏ c. when touched.

5. Plants change position
   - ❏ a. when offered food.
   - ❏ b. as they grow.
   - ❏ c. while they sleep.

Understanding Ideas

6. Plants and animals
   - ❏ a. try to move when they are touched.
   - ❏ b. eat.
   - ❏ c. respond to their surroundings.

7. You can conclude from the article that food
   - ❏ a. serves the same purpose for animals and plants.
   - ❏ b. is made by both plants and animals.
   - ❏ c. is eaten by both plants and animals.

8. Plants and animals reproduce
   - ❏ a. in the same way.
   - ❏ b. from seeds and bulbs.
   - ❏ c. in different ways.

9. Using food and moving are tests that apply
   - ❏ a. to all living things.
   - ❏ b. only to plants.
   - ❏ c. only to animals.

10. You can conclude from the article that sunlight
    - ❏ a. is important to plants.
    - ❏ b. is a requirement for life.
    - ❏ c. causes growth in animals.

A Plantlike Animal

If you walk along a rocky beach at low tide, you may not notice the sea anemones. When they are dry, anemones look like rocks. When they are underwater, they open up and look like flowering plants. They have thick stalks and "petals." But anemones are not rocks or plants; they are animals.

The anemone's petals are really poison-tipped tentacles. When a small fish swims too close to the anemone, its tentacles close around the fish and pull it inside. Then the anemone digests its meal.

People used to think that all sea anemones did was sit and wait for food to come by. But it seems that anemones are more complicated than that. An anemone sprouts buds that become new anemones. Eventually, the anemones form groups. If two groups begin to crowd each other, an anemone war can develop.

An anemone from one group can use its poison tentacles to slap an anemone from the other group. The other anemone can slap back. When the fighting gets serious, the loser may "run away." It slithers out of its enemy's reach.

It's not known yet whether anemones have other ways of getting and keeping territory, but scientists are considering further research.

1. **Recognizing Words in Context**

   Find the word *slithers* in the passage. One definition below is a *synonym* for that word; it means the same or almost the same thing. One definition is an *antonym*; it has the opposite or nearly opposite meaning. The other has a completely different meaning. Label the definitions S for *synonym*, A for *antonym*, and D for *different*.

   _____ a. stays

   _____ b. slides

   _____ c. glows

2. **Distinguishing Fact from Opinion**

   Two of the statements below present *facts*, which can be proved correct. The other statement is an *opinion*, which expresses someone's thoughts or beliefs. Label the statements F for *fact* and O for *opinion*.

   _____ a. Anemones are animals.

   _____ b. Anemones' tentacles have poison tips.

   _____ c. Sea anemones just sit, waiting for food to come by.

3. **Keeping Events in Order**

   Label the statements below 1, 2, and 3 to show the order in which the events happened.

   _____ a. The losing anemone runs away.

   _____ b. One anemone slaps the other with its tentacles.

   _____ c. Sea anemone groups become crowded.

4. **Making Correct Inferences**

   Two of the statements below are correct *inferences,* or reasonable guesses. They are based on information in the passage. The other statement is an incorrect, or faulty, inference. Label the statements C for *correct* inference and F for *faulty* inference.

   _____ a. Sea anemones are more active than people once thought.

   _____ b. Sea anemones can think.

   _____ c. Sea anemones fight for space when they become crowded.

5. **Understanding Main Ideas**

   One of the statements below expresses the main idea of the passage. One statement is too general, or too broad. The other explains only part of the passage; it is too narrow. Label the statements M for *main idea,* B for *too broad,* and N for *too narrow.*

   _____ a. Some sea creatures are very strange.

   _____ b. One sea anemone uses its tentacles to slap another anemone.

   _____ c. Besides catching food, sea anemones often fight for space in which to live.

Correct Answers, Part A _____

Correct Answers, Part B _____

Total Correct Answers _____

3 A A Western Roundup

Newborn calves have to be branded before they leave their mothers. Otherwise, no one could tell to which ranch they belonged. This was the reason for the spring, or calf, roundup. The ranchers of each district joined for this task. With their cowhands, they met at some appointed place. A roundup boss, or foreman, was chosen. It was the foreman's duty to supervise the work. The riders, in twos or threes, moved out over the range with orders to drive in the cattle to the roundup ground.

Sometimes this job took several days. The cattle were wild. Often they were found in rough country where riding was difficult. As each group of cattle came in, they were sometimes driven into corrals, or great circles of wooden fence. More often the cattle were kept in the open and guarded. The riders picked for that job circled the herd and drove back any cattle that tried to break away.

The job of branding then began. Expert ropers caught the calves with a loop around their hind legs. They then dragged the calves out of the herd to the fires where the branding irons were heating. A pair of wrestlers seized each calf, threw it on its side, and turned loose the rope. The roper called out the brand that was on the calf's mother. This mark was then stamped on the calf. Certain "earmarks" might be cut, which would later help distinguish the animal when it was crowded too close in a herd for its brand to be visible. The calf was then allowed to find its way back to its mother.

It was a lively scene. The calves kicked and bawled. Workers ran with irons that had to be used quickly before they cooled. Clouds of dust from the milling herd and the galloping riders mingled with the blue smoke of burning logs.

Tenderfeet, to whom the scene at first might have seemed cruel, would have been surprised to see how rapidly the calves recovered. Neither the cowhands nor the cattle owners wished to be brutal.

Often some of the animals evaded the spring roundup. The calves among them grew up and separated from their mothers without a brand to tell who owned them. These were the mavericks. As ownership was determined by the brand, the name *maverick* came to be given to all unmarked calves caught straying from the herd.

Reading Time _____

Recalling Facts

1. A roundup boss is called a
   - ❏ a. rider.
   - ❏ b. foreman.
   - ❏ c. cowhand.

2. Calves are branded so that
   - ❏ a. ownership can be determined.
   - ❏ b. they can find their mothers.
   - ❏ c. they can be fed.

3. A calf's brand is
   - ❏ a. one of a kind.
   - ❏ b. the same as its mother's.
   - ❏ c. changed every five years.

4. Newborn calves have to be branded
   - ❏ a. after they leave their mothers.
   - ❏ b. before they leave their mothers.
   - ❏ c. right after birth.

5. In order to be branded, calves are
   - ❏ a. roped together.
   - ❏ b. driven into the herd.
   - ❏ c. roped and dragged from the herd.

Understanding Ideas

6. Using hot irons to brand calves makes sure that
   - ❏ a. the brands are permanent.
   - ❏ b. the calves live in herds.
   - ❏ c. the calves run away.

7. You can conclude from the article that tenderfeet are
   - ❏ a. people with sore feet.
   - ❏ b. those who know little about cattle and herding.
   - ❏ c. seasoned cowhands.

8. It is likely that maverick calves
   - ❏ a. could not be branded.
   - ❏ b. were claimed by anyone who caught them.
   - ❏ c. were killed by wild animals.

9. It is likely that calves were branded
   - ❏ a. on their stomachs.
   - ❏ b. wherever the branding iron landed.
   - ❏ c. where the brand could be clearly seen.

10. When used to describe a person, the word *maverick* means
    - ❏ a. independent.
    - ❏ b. shy.
    - ❏ c. lazy.

3 B Choosing a Brand

The Adams family sat around the kitchen table in their new ranch house. They had just moved to Texas from the East and bought five hundred head of cattle. "We have to brand the cattle right away," Mr. Adams said. "That way, we can prove which ones are ours."

"I heard that our neighbor, Sam Maverick, refuses to brand his cattle," Mrs. Adams said. "He thinks it's cruel."

"Maverick's a fool!" Mr. Adams said. "With herds roaming freely on the open range, the cattle get all mixed up. Using brands is the only way to tell them apart. What do you think would be the best brand for our family?"

"With all the walking we have to do, how about an *A* with feet on it— the Walking A Ranch?" suggested Sally Adams.

"I think it should be an *E* lying on its side for Ethan—the Lazy E Ranch," joked Seth, referring to his younger brother. Ethan gave Seth a shove.

"Now, now, children," said Mrs. Adams. "We're here in a strange new place, miles and miles from our nearest neighbor. We have to stick together as a family. I think our brand should show that we're united in this adventure. I suggest a circle with the letter *A* in the middle—the Circle A Ranch."

The Circle A Ranch it was.

1. Recognizing Words in Context

Find the word *freely* in the passage. One definition below is a *synonym* for that word; it means the same or almost the same thing. One definition is an *antonym;* it has the opposite or nearly opposite meaning. The other has a completely different meaning. Label the definitions S for *synonym,* A for *antonym,* and D for *different.*

_____ a. costly

_____ b. loosely

_____ c. confined

2. Distinguishing Fact from Opinion

Two of the statements below present *facts,* which can be proved correct. The other statement is an *opinion,* which expresses someone's thoughts or beliefs. Label the statements F for *fact* and O for *opinion.*

_____ a. Sam Maverick was foolish not to brand his cattle.

_____ b. The Adams family had bought five hundred head of cattle.

_____ c. Branding was the only way to prove ownership of cattle.

3. Keeping Events in Order

Label the statements below 1, 2, and 3 to show the order in which the events happened.

_____ a. They became the Circle A Ranch.

_____ b. The Adams family moved to Texas.

_____ c. Sally wanted to name the ranch the Walking A.

4. Making Correct Inferences

Two of the statements below are correct *inferences*, or reasonable guesses. They are based on information in the passage. The other statement is an incorrect, or faulty, inference. Label the statements C for *correct* inference and F for *faulty* inference.

_____ a. Sam Maverick did not care whether he lost some of his cattle.

_____ b. Everyone in the family liked the name Circle A Ranch.

_____ c. Seth liked to tease Ethan.

5. Understanding Main Ideas

One of the statements below expresses the main idea of the passage. One statement is too general, or too broad. The other explains only part of the passage; it is too narrow. Label the statements M for *main idea*, B for *too broad*, and N for *too narrow*.

_____ a. Every western rancher had a different, distinctive brand.

_____ b. The Adams family wanted to choose a brand that would be a good symbol for their family and their new life.

_____ c. An *E* lying on its side stands for "lazy E."

Correct Answers, Part A _____

Correct Answers, Part B _____

Total Correct Answers _____

The Sandhill Crane

Through the still waters of an open marsh, the sandhill crane wades on stiltlike legs. Its long neck erect, it scans with keen eyes for signs of danger. Then it lowers its head and searches the water. Out darts its neck, and its long daggerlike beak holds a frog or a salamander. The crane swallows its catch in one or two gulps. At other times, it seems to prefer dry land and can be seen in the fields, catching lizards, mice, and grasshoppers or making a meal of grain.

A wary bird, the sandhill crane detects the faintest sound or sight of danger. With a few long running strides, it takes slowly to the air, flapping its wings in a lazy rhythm. It always flies with its neck and legs stretched out in line with its body. At the same time, it utters a booming call that can be heard long after it has flown out of sight.

In spring, the male cranes bow and strut before the females. This is their dance of courtship. The female lays only two or, rarely, three eggs a season. The nest is often no more than a basin in the ground, lined with grass and weed stems. When the young hatch, they are covered with a full coat of soft, fluffy down. They are sturdy and can run about within a few hours after hatching. When autumn comes, they are strong enough to join the long flight to their winter grounds with the adults.

Cranes are often mistaken for herons, but they differ in several ways. The crane has compact plumage that grows close to its body and looks almost smooth. The heron has fluffy plumage and long, fine feathers that give it a wispy appearance. Both birds have three front toes and one back toe. The back toe of the crane is higher on the leg than the front toes. All the toes of the heron are on the same level. When a crane flies, it stretches its neck forward and holds it straight out in front. The heron folds its neck so that its head is pulled back and held close to its body.

The two subspecies of the sandhill crane are the Florida crane and the little brown crane. Sandhill cranes were long threatened by extinction. Strict conservation laws and the establishment of protected areas for breeding have saved these birds.

Reading Time _____

Recalling Facts

1. The sandhill crane's legs are
   - ❏ a. long and thin like stilts.
   - ❏ b. short and heavy.
   - ❏ c. used for catching food.

2. The crane's beak is
   - ❏ a. rounded at the tip.
   - ❏ b. long and daggerlike.
   - ❏ c. short and pointed.

3. Mating season for the sandhill crane occurs
   - ❏ a. during the fall.
   - ❏ b. in the spring.
   - ❏ c. in the winter.

4. Cranes are often mistaken for
   - ❏ a. crows.
   - ❏ b. seagulls.
   - ❏ c. herons.

5. Two subspecies of the sandhill crane are the little brown crane and the
   - ❏ a. Florida crane.
   - ❏ b. Louisiana crane.
   - ❏ c. Texas crane.

Understanding Ideas

6. It is likely that the shape of the crane's beak
   - ❏ a. helps it catch food.
   - ❏ b. helps it swallow.
   - ❏ c. aids in flying.

7. You can conclude from the article that cranes mate in the spring
   - ❏ a. so that the young will be strong enough to fly by autumn.
   - ❏ b. because the weather is warmer.
   - ❏ c. because more food is available.

8. If you see a tall, long-legged bird with wispy-looking feathers, it is probably a
   - ❏ a. crow
   - ❏ b. crane.
   - ❏ c. heron.

9. The number of sandhill cranes is
   - ❏ a. probably growing smaller.
   - ❏ b. probably growing larger.
   - ❏ c. the same as it has been for many years.

10. It is likely that without conservation laws, the sandhill crane would have
    - ❏ a. stopped breeding.
    - ❏ b. died out.
    - ❏ c. run out of food.

The Frogs Who Wanted a King

The frogs had always lived a happy, carefree life. They jumped and splashed in the water without a worry. Some frogs, however, thought they should have a king to rule over them. So they asked Jupiter to send them a king.

Jupiter thought the idea of the frogs wanting a king was very funny. As a joke, he threw a log into the lake. "Here's your king," he rumbled in his deep voice. The log landed with a great splash that sent all the frogs scampering for safety.

After a while, one brave little frog saw that the log did not move. He jumped closer and closer to it, but still the log did not move. Soon all the frogs were jumping and splashing around the log as if it were not there.

The frogs who wanted a king approached Jupiter again. "We want a real king," they said, "one who will really rule over us."

Jupiter was tired of the frogs' complaints, and so he sent them a crane for a king. The crane at once began to snap up frogs and swallow them down. The frogs who survived begged Jupiter to take the king back. "You're the ones who wanted a king," Jupiter replied. "Now you have to make the best of what you asked for!"

1. **Recognizing Words in Context**

   Find the word *deep* in the passage. One definition below is a *synonym* for that word; it means the same or almost the same thing. One definition is an *antonym*; it has the opposite or nearly opposite meaning. The other has a completely different meaning. Label the definitions S for *synonym*, A for *antonym*, and D for *different*.

   _____ a. low-pitched

   _____ b. high-pitched

   _____ c. sunken

2. **Distinguishing Fact from Opinion**

   Two of the statements below present *facts*, which can be proved correct. The other statement is an *opinion*, which expresses someone's thoughts or beliefs. Label the statements F for *fact* and O for *opinion*.

   _____ a. The crane snapped up and swallowed the frogs.

   _____ b. The frogs did not think the log was a good enough king.

   _____ c. Some frogs wanted a king.

3. **Keeping Events in Order**

   Label the statements below 1, 2, and 3 to show the order in which the events happened.

   _____ a. Jupiter gave the frogs a log for a king.

   _____ b. Jupiter sent a crane to be the frogs' king.

   _____ c. The frogs asked Jupiter to send them a king.

4. **Making Correct Inferences**

   Two of the statements below are correct *inferences,* or reasonable guesses. They are based on information in the passage. The other statement is an incorrect, or faulty, inference. Label the statements C for *correct* inference and F for *faulty* inference.

   _____ a. Jupiter did not take the frogs very seriously.

   _____ b. Frogs are a favorite food of cranes.

   _____ c. The frogs needed a real king.

5. **Understanding Main Ideas**

   One of the statements below expresses the main idea of the passage. One statement is too general, or too broad. The other explains only part of the passage; it is too narrow. Label the statements M for *main idea,* B for *too broad,* and N for *too narrow.*

   _____ a. Jupiter sent a crane to be the frogs' king.

   _____ b. Cranes are the natural enemies of frogs.

   _____ c. The frogs wanted a king, but they should have let well enough alone.

Correct Answers, Part A _____

Correct Answers, Part B _____

Total Correct Answers _____

The Legend of Robin Hood

Whether he was a living man or only a legend is uncertain. Old ballads tell of Robin Hood and his followers who roamed Sherwood Forest, near Nottingham, in central England. There they lived a carefree life. They passed the time playing games of archery, hunting the king's deer, and robbing the rich. Legend says they shared their spoils with the poor.

Robin Hood probably became an outlaw by killing a deer on the king's land. Then he had killed one of the king's foresters who threatened his life. A price was set on Robin's head, and he went into hiding. Soon there gathered about him other bold people who had been outlawed. Some of them hated the hard rule of the barons. Others loved the free life of the outdoors. More than once someone won a place in the band by defeating Robin himself in a fair fight.

One day, when Robin was about to cross a narrow bridge, a stranger seven feet (2.1 meters) tall blocked the way. The two men fought with quarterstaves (long, stout sticks), and Robin Hood was knocked into the stream. Robin Hood praised this stranger and asked him to join his band. Little John became Robin Hood's right-hand man.

In later ballads, Robin's sweetheart, Maid Marian, was introduced. When Robin Hood was outlawed, she dressed as a page and went to seek him. At last, they met. Both were disguised, and neither recognized the other. They fought until Robin, admiring her skill, invited Marian to join his band. Then she recognized his voice.

Robin Hood's enemy was the sheriff of Nottingham. The sheriff tried by force and trickery to bring the outlaw to justice. He was always outwitted. He even announced a shooting match, feeling sure that Robin Hood would appear to show his skill with the bow. Robin did appear, but in disguise. He won the prize, a golden arrow. It was handed to Robin by the sheriff himself. Not until Robin was once more safe in Sherwood Forest did the sheriff learn how he had been deceived.

The Robin Hood legends may have grown up about an actual victim of the harsh forest laws of old England. Robin Hood is said to have lived from 1160 to 1247. Most legends say that Robin Hood died at Kirklees Priory in Yorkshire. Near the ruins of this priory is a grave supposed to be Robin's.

Reading Time _____

Recalling Facts

1. Robin Hood met his friend Little John
   - ❏ a. during a war.
   - ❏ b. at a fair.
   - ❏ c. on a bridge.

2. Robin Hood probably became an outlaw by
   - ❏ a. robbing the rich.
   - ❏ b. killing the king's deer.
   - ❏ c. living in Sherwood Forest.

3. Quarterstaves are
   - ❏ a. used to build houses.
   - ❏ b. used to build bridges.
   - ❏ c. long, stout sticks.

4. Maid Marian was
   - ❏ a. the sheriff of Nottingham.
   - ❏ b. Robin Hood's sweetheart.
   - ❏ c. the Queen.

5. The story of Robin Hood is told in
   - ❏ a. the Bible.
   - ❏ b. atlases.
   - ❏ c. old ballads.

Understanding Ideas

6. Stories about Robin Hood are still told today, which suggests that
   - ❏ a. people like the stories.
   - ❏ b. people have forgotten the stories.
   - ❏ c. the stories are based on fact.

7. You can conclude from the article that Robin Hood
   - ❏ a. was a real person.
   - ❏ b. was a legend.
   - ❏ c. may have been a real person or a legend.

8. The article suggests that Robin Hood was
   - ❏ a. impressed by fighting skills.
   - ❏ b. was often outwitted.
   - ❏ c. not a very good archer.

9. The article suggests that the sheriff of Nottingham was
   - ❏ a. a brilliant man.
   - ❏ b. easily fooled.
   - ❏ c. dishonest.

10. You can conclude from the article that Robin Hood was
    - ❏ a. a greedy person.
    - ❏ b. an unfair fighter.
    - ❏ c. a skilled archer.

Sheriff in the Greenwood

One day, Little John, one of Robin Hood's band, saw the sheriff of Nottingham hunting in Sherwood Forest. Little John stopped the sheriff and his party. First, he stole the sheriff's silver. Then he persuaded the sheriff's cook to come with him to Robin's camp. Finally, Little John accosted the sheriff and offered to lead him to a large herd of deer.

With the sheriff following him, Little John galloped into Robin's camp deep in the forest. The sheriff was terrified, but all Robin did was invite him to stay for dinner. The sheriff's own cook prepared the meal and served it on the sheriff's own silver plates. Purple with rage, the hungry sheriff could hardly eat the meal. Used to sleeping in a soft bed, he did not sleep a wink on the hard ground.

In the morning, Robin cheerfully announced his plan to keep the sheriff in his camp for a year. The sheriff, cold and miserable and hungry, said he would rather die. So Robin agreed to let him go, but the sheriff had to swear that he would never harm Robin or his followers.

With no intention of ever keeping his promise, the sheriff gladly swore the oath, and Robin set the humiliated sheriff on the road back to Nottingham.

1. **Recognizing Words in Context**

   Find the word *accosted* in the passage. One definition below is a *synonym* for that word; it means the same or almost the same thing. One definition is an *antonym;* it has the opposite or nearly opposite meaning. The other has a completely different meaning. Label the definitions S for *synonym*, A for *antonym*, and D for *different*.

   _____ a. accompanied

   _____ b. approached

   _____ c. ignored

2. **Distinguishing Fact from Opinion**

   Two of the statements below present *facts*, which can be proved correct. The other statement is an *opinion*, which expresses someone's thoughts or beliefs. Label the statements F for *fact* and O for *opinion*.

   _____ a. Little John stole the sheriff's silver.

   _____ b. The sheriff had no intention of keeping his promise.

   _____ c. Robin announced his plan to keep the sheriff in his camp for a year.

3. Keeping Events in Order

Label the statements below 1, 2, and 3 to show the order in which the events happened.

_____ a. The sheriff swore not to harm Robin or his followers.

_____ b. Robin invited the sheriff to have dinner with him and his followers.

_____ c. Little John offered to lead the sheriff to a herd of deer.

4. Making Correct Inferences

Two of the statements below are correct *inferences,* or reasonable guesses. They are based on information in the passage. The other statement is an incorrect, or faulty, inference. Label the statements C for *correct* inference and F for *faulty* inference.

_____ a. The sheriff was an honorable man.

_____ b. Robin Hood was cleverer than the sheriff.

_____ c. The sheriff was soft and cowardly.

5. Understanding Main Ideas

One of the statements below expresses the main idea of the passage. One statement is too general, or too broad. The other explains only part of the passage; it is too narrow. Label the statements M for *main idea,* B for *too broad,* and N for *too narrow.*

_____ a. Little John captured the sheriff of Nottingham and led him to Robin's camp.

_____ b. Robin Hood humiliated the sheriff of Nottingham by treating him with courtesy.

_____ c. Robin Hood and the sheriff of Nottingham met.

Correct Answers, Part A _____

Correct Answers, Part B _____

Total Correct Answers _____

Save the Watershed

A watershed is the area drained by a river or a stream. Such an area slopes toward a common land trough. Some rain runs off, or drains, over the ground surface. Runoff water forms small streams, which flow into larger ones. These in time join to form rivers.

A natural watershed conserves water. It has clear streams and a cover of trees, grasses, and other plants. Plants help form a part of the topsoil called humus. Humus consists of rotting leaves and wood, germs, dead insects, and other plant and animal remains. It provides some of the nutrients for new plant life. Along with a network of roots, humus acts as a blotter that soaks up rain. Plants break the force of falling rain and scatter the drops over leaves and branches. Some of the water returns to the air by evaporation. Some of the water used by plants is passed through their leaves into the air again by transpiration. The rest of the water sinks into the earth through countless tiny channels. Some of the spaces through which water drains are caused by natural features of the land or soil itself. Others are made by plant roots and burrowing animals like earthworms, insects, and moles.

The level at which the earth is for all time saturated is known as the water table. This vast water supply under the ground changes with the seasons and the amount of rainfall. During long, heavy rains, the soil may not be able to soak up all the water. Some of it runs off the surface. In a forest watershed, it moves slowly. Deep snow that melts slowly allows water to soak into the soil gradually.

Sometimes trees in an area have been cut down due to poor forestry practices. Grasses and other plants may have been stripped off by fire, over-grazing, or poor farming practices. The water from rainfall then flows over the ground instead of being absorbed by the plant growth that once was there.

Mud closes the channels through which water sinks into the soil. If the land is level, the water stands in stagnant pools. If it slopes, the water runs downhill into the rivers. Streams become brown with silt because the racing water carries soil along with it. In the spring, heavy rains and melting snows overflow the riverbanks. In the summer, streams, springs, and wells can dry up.

Reading Time _____

Recalling Facts

1. A watershed is
   - ❏ a. a river or stream.
   - ❏ b. the area at the mouth of a river.
   - ❏ c. the area drained by a river or a stream.

2. A natural watershed
   - ❏ a. creates a waterfall.
   - ❏ b. conserves water.
   - ❏ c. provides the power for electricity.

3. The level at which the earth is for all time saturated is known as
   - ❏ a. the water table.
   - ❏ b. humus.
   - ❏ c. a natural watershed.

4. The underground supply of water changes with the seasons and
   - ❏ a. water conservation.
   - ❏ b. the amount of rainfall.
   - ❏ c. the tilt of the Earth.

5. If land slopes, water
   - ❏ a. runs downhill into rivers.
   - ❏ b. becomes stagnant.
   - ❏ c. evaporates more quickly.

Understanding Ideas

6. Water moves slowly over the surface of a forest watershed because
   - ❏ a. there are no plants to absorb the water.
   - ❏ b. plant growth absorbs the water gradually.
   - ❏ c. fences stem the flow.

7. Watersheds are important to
   - ❏ a. wildlife preservation.
   - ❏ b. industrial pollution.
   - ❏ c. water conservation.

8. You can conclude from the article that silt
   - ❏ a. is a part of the soil.
   - ❏ b. is dangerous to plants and animals.
   - ❏ c. causes water to stagnate.

9. It is likely that without watersheds,
   - ❏ a. there would be no drinkable water.
   - ❏ b. rivers and streams would dry up.
   - ❏ c. the water supply would decrease.

10. For their water supply, watersheds depend on
    - ❏ a. rain and snow.
    - ❏ b. rivers and streams.
    - ❏ c. humus.

The Year the Nile Failed

For thousands of years, Egypt, a country in northern Africa, depended for its life on the rise and fall of the Nile River. The annual flooding of the Nile left behind rich silt that covered the land the farmers cultivated.

In the spring of the year 1200, something out of the ordinary happened. The Nile turned green and had a bad smell. Its waters were found to be choked with plant matter. A scientist named Abd al-Latif determined that the condition was caused by a shortage of rainfall in the Nile's watershed—the source of the river's waters—far to the south.

That summer the Nile failed to rise and flood. Without the life-giving floodwaters to enrich the soil, the land became parched and barren. Crops failed. Famine ruled Egypt.

In April 1201, the Nile again turned green and smelly. Again the river failed to rise and flood. Egypt began a second year of famine with few resources. Between July 1200 and April 1202, more than 100,000 Egyptians died of hunger and disease. Latif wrote at the time, "They carried away, particularly from Cairo, each day between 100 and 500 dead bodies."

Finally, in September 1202, the Nile River rose and flooded once more. After two years, the threat of famine left Egypt—at least for the moment.

1. **Recognizing Words in Context**

   Find the word *rose* in the passage. One definition below is a *synonym* for that word; it means the same or almost the same thing. One definition is an *antonym*; it has the opposite or nearly opposite meaning. The other has a completely different meaning. Label the definitions S for *synonym*, A for *antonym*, and D for *different*.

   _____ a. sank

   _____ b. flower

   _____ c. grew

2. **Distinguishing Fact from Opinion**

   Two of the statements below present *facts*, which can be proved correct. The other statement is an *opinion*, which expresses someone's thoughts or beliefs. Label the statements F for *fact* and O for *opinion*.

   _____ a. More than 100,000 Egyptians died during the two years of famine.

   _____ b. The Egyptians should not have been so dependent on the Nile.

   _____ c. In the years 1200 and 1201, the Nile failed to rise and flood.

3. Keeping Events in Order

Label the statements below 1, 2, and 3 to show the order in which the events happened.

_____ a. The waters of the Nile turned green and smelly.

_____ b. Famine ruled Egypt.

_____ c. That summer the river did not rise.

4. Making Correct Inferences

Two of the statements below are correct *inferences,* or reasonable guesses. They are based on information in the passage. The other statement is an incorrect, or faulty, inference. Label the statements C for *correct* inference and F for *faulty* inference.

_____ a. Crops could not grow without the silt that the floodwaters left behind.

_____ b. The rise and fall of the Nile were dependent on the amount of rainfall at the river's source.

_____ c. In the past, the Nile had never failed to rise.

5. Understanding Main Ideas

One of the statements below expresses the main idea of the passage. One statement is too general, or too broad. The other explains only part of the passage; it is too narrow. Label the statements M for *main idea,* B for *too broad,* and N for *too narrow.*

_____ a. Without the Nile River, Egypt would be a desert.

_____ b. In the spring of 1200, the Nile River turned green and smelled bad.

_____ c. When the Nile River failed to rise for two years in a row, famine and disease killed many Egyptians.

Correct Answers, Part A _____

Correct Answers, Part B _____

Total Correct Answers _____

Peale: Patriot and Painter

Charles Willson Peale was a painter. He was also the brother, father, uncle, and teacher of painters. He and his family painted many pictures of George Washington and other famous Americans. But Peale never even saw a painting until he was a grown man.

Peale was a saddlemaker in Annapolis, Maryland. He did watchmaking and silversmithing on the side. One day he went to Norfolk for leather supplies, and there he saw paintings for the first time. If the pictures had been good, Peale might never have thought of becoming a painter himself. But they were very bad. He was sure he could do better. When he returned home, he began to paint. He found that he could make money at it. He decided to make painting his trade.

Peale went to London to study with Benjamin West, a well-known artist. Peale was already a patriot. He wanted the colonies to break away from England.

In 1772, Peale visited Mount Vernon. There he painted the first known picture of George Washington.

When the Revolutionary War started, Peale took his family to Philadelphia. He was made captain of a company of volunteers. His company fought at Trenton and Princeton. Peale was an unusual soldier. He carried paints as well as a musket. If his men were hungry, he would cook them a meal. If their boots wore out, he made them moccasins. If he had nothing else to do, he painted miniature pictures of his officers.

Many of Peale's ideas were ahead of his time. He believed that all men were created equal. He hated slavery and freed the slaves he had inherited. He thought that girls as well as boys should be educated. He also believed that if people took care of themselves, they could live to be 112.

When Peale reached the age of eighty-six, it looked as though he might indeed live to be 112. But one day, in the middle of the winter of 1827, he did something that could have killed a man half his age. Cold and tired, he carried a trunk on his back for a whole mile just to save a little time. The strain on his heart was too great. He lived for only a few months after that.

A man of ideas and a patriot, Peale helped make history. He left behind paintings that are a record of a young America.

Reading Time _____

Recalling Facts

1. Charles Willson Peale's first trade was
   - ❑ a. farming.
   - ❑ b. sailing.
   - ❑ c. saddlemaking.

2. The first known painting of George Washington was painted
   - ❑ a. at Mount Vernon.
   - ❑ b. in Washington, D.C.
   - ❑ c. in Annapolis, Maryland.

3. Peale took part in the Revolutionary War as a
   - ❑ a. captain.
   - ❑ b. general.
   - ❑ c. doctor.

4. During the war, Peale also worked as
   - ❑ a. a silversmith and a cook.
   - ❑ b. a cook and a cobbler.
   - ❑ c. a cobbler and a watchmaker.

5. Peale died
   - ❑ a. at a young age.
   - ❑ b. while fighting for his country.
   - ❑ c. when he was eighty-six.

Understanding Ideas

6. The article suggests that Peale came from
   - ❑ a. a very wealthy family.
   - ❑ b. a middle class background.
   - ❑ c. royalty.

7. You can conclude from the article that a patriot is someone who
   - ❑ a. is loyal.
   - ❑ b. believes in war.
   - ❑ c. loves and supports his or her country.

8. According to the article, Peale's death was a result of
   - ❑ a. poor judgment.
   - ❑ b. bad luck.
   - ❑ c. laziness.

9. Peale might be described as a
   - ❑ a. free thinker.
   - ❑ b. bookworm.
   - ❑ c. follower.

10. The article suggests that Peale was
    - ❑ a. an ordinary man.
    - ❑ b. a man to be admired.
    - ❑ c. the outstanding artist of his time.

Unfinished Painting

Charles Willson Peale painted the first known picture of George Washington. The most famous picture of Washington, however, was painted by Gilbert Stuart. He was the leading American portrait painter in the late 1700s. It was Washington's wife, Martha, who commissioned Stuart to paint a portrait of her husband. Look at the picture of Washington on a dollar bill. Stuart's painting of the president served as a model for that picture.

Gilbert Stuart never finished his painting of George Washington. If he had finished the picture, he would have had to turn it over to the Washingtons. But Stuart hoped to make his fortune from painting Washington. Instead of finishing the portrait, Stuart kept it in order to make copies of it. Photographs did not exist in the 1700s. If you wanted a picture of someone, you had it painted by an artist. Stuart made and sold 70 copies of his unfinished portrait of George Washington. Because he charged $100 for each copy, he called these paintings his "hundred-dollar bills"!

Washington tried to get Stuart to give him the painting. He even went to the artist's studio to demand it. However, Stuart never released the painting to its subject. The portrait of Washington was still in Stuart's studio when the artist died in 1828. And it was still unfinished.

1. **Recognizing Words in Context**

   Find the word *charged* in the passage. One definition below is a *synonym* for that word; it means the same or almost the same thing. One definition is an *antonym;* it has the opposite or nearly opposite meaning. The other has a completely different meaning. Label the definitions S for *synonym*, A for *antonym*, and D for *different*.

   _____ a. asked

   _____ b. accused

   _____ c. gave

2. **Distinguishing Fact from Opinion**

   Two of the statements below present *facts*, which can be proved correct. The other statement is an *opinion*, which expresses someone's thoughts or beliefs. Label the statements F for *fact* and O for *opinion*.

   _____ a. Gilbert Stuart never finished his portrait of George Washington.

   _____ b. Gilbert Stuart's portrait of George Washington served as a model for the picture of Washington on a dollar bill.

   _____ c. It was dishonest of Stuart to keep the painting so that he could copy it.

3. Keeping Events in Order

Label the statements below 1, 2, and 3 to show the order in which the events happened.

_____ a. Martha Washington commissioned Gilbert Stuart to paint a portrait of her husband, George.

_____ b. Gilbert Stuart made and sold copies of the portrait of Washington.

_____ c. The unfinished painting remained in the artist's studio until his death.

4. Making Correct Inferences

Two of the statements below are correct *inferences*, or reasonable guesses. They are based on information in the passage. The other statement is an incorrect, or faulty, inference. Label the statements C for *correct* inference and F for *faulty* inference.

_____ a. Copies of Gilbert Stuart's painting of George Washington were in great demand.

_____ b. After Stuart's death, Washington had the painting finished by another artist.

_____ c. Stuart was more interested in making money than in pleasing Washington.

5. Understanding Main Ideas

One of the statements below expresses the main idea of the passage. One statement is too general, or too broad. The other explains only part of the passage; it is too narrow. Label the statements M for *main idea*, B for *too broad*, and N for *too narrow*.

_____ a. Gilbert Stuart (1755–1828) was perhaps America's leading portrait artist.

_____ b. Gilbert Stuart charged $100 each for copies of his portrait of George Washington.

_____ c. The most famous painting of George Washington, by Gilbert Stuart, was never finished by the artist.

Correct Answers, Part A _____

Correct Answers, Part B _____

Total Correct Answers _____

Colors

One of the most striking features of the visible world is the abundance of color. The sky can be blue or black or gray or even reddish or purplish. Soils can be black or brown or gray or even red. Bodies of water look blue or green. One of the important ways people obtain information about the world is by looking at the colors of things. When the green leaves of a plant turn brown, it may be a sign that the plant is sick. It can also be a sign of the season of year. In the autumn, the leaves of many trees turn brown.

The color of a fruit can reveal whether it is ripe. A green banana is unripe; a yellow one is ripe. A yellow banana with brown and black spots is overripe. A green tomato is unripe, but a red one is ripe. Color can also indicate the flavor of foods. Brown rice has a different flavor from that of white rice.

What does it mean to say that a tomato is red? Is color part of the tomato in the same way that shape is? A tomato examined in the dark is still perceived as round but not as being red. It has no color at all. Moreover, if a bright blue light is shone only on the tomato, it does not look red but black. So color, unlike shape, depends on light. In fact, it cannot exist apart from light.

Light from the noontime sun looks white. But if a ray of white light is aimed at a prism, a broad band of different colors looking like a rainbow emerges. This color array is called the visible spectrum.

In the seventeenth century, Isaac Newton discovered that a second prism could not add more color to light that had already passed through a prism. Red stayed red, green stayed green, and so on. But he observed that the second prism could spread the colors of the spectrum farther apart. A narrow red beam entering the second prism would emerge as a wider band of red. Newton also found that if he turned the second prism upside down, white light would emerge. From these experiments he concluded that white light is a mixture of many different colors. A prism is somehow able to bend it in such a way that the individual colors separate.

Reading Time _____

Recalling Facts

1. Color cannot exist apart from
   - ❑ a. shape.
   - ❑ b. the sun.
   - ❑ c. light.

2. Color can indicate whether a plant
   - ❑ a. has shape.
   - ❑ b. is sick.
   - ❑ c. bears fruit.

3. White light is
   - ❑ a. the absence of color.
   - ❑ b. a mixture of many different colors.
   - ❑ c. a mixture of three colors.

4. A rainbow-like band of different colors is called
   - ❑ a. the visible spectrum.
   - ❑ b. a prism.
   - ❑ c. reflected light.

5. The seventeenth-century scientist who experimented with light was
   - ❑ a. Richard Isaac.
   - ❑ b. Isaac Newton.
   - ❑ c. Thomas Edison.

Understanding Ideas

6. Without color, the visible world would be
   - ❑ a. invisible.
   - ❑ b. less interesting.
   - ❑ c. shapeless.

7. You can conclude from the article that before Newton's experiments, white light was thought to be
   - ❑ a. prismatic.
   - ❑ b. blue.
   - ❑ c. white.

8. You can conclude from the article that light
   - ❑ a. gives objects their shape.
   - ❑ b. gives objects their color.
   - ❑ c. determines the size of an object.

9. In the dark, an orange carrot would be
   - ❑ a. orange.
   - ❑ b. black.
   - ❑ c. colorless.

10. The rainbow that sometimes appears after a storm is the result of sunlight aimed at water droplets, which suggests that water droplets act as a
    - ❑ a. prism.
    - ❑ b. visible spectrum.
    - ❑ c. microscope.

Seeing in Color

In the 1800s, an Englishman named John Dalton realized that he was not seeing color the way other people were. To Dalton, red and green looked the same. When he looked at a pink flower in the daylight, he saw a blue flower. But that same pink flower looked red by candlelight.

Dalton began to study what we now call color blindness. He was the first to do so. Dalton thought that the problem must be with the fluid inside his eyes. Other people's eye fluid, he decided, was clear, so they saw colors correctly. His eye fluid must be blue, modifying everything he saw. As it turned out, Dalton was wrong, but his study interested other people in the question of how we see colors.

Today we know that color vision depends on structures within the eye that are sensitive to waves of light. Some pick up short waves of light, others pick up medium waves, and still others pick up long waves. If the structure for one kind is missing, the person cannot see certain colors. Modern researchers now know that John Dalton had a medium-wavelength problem. People missing structures for that kind of wavelength see pink flowers as blue in daylight.

1. **Recognizing Words in Context**

   Find the word *modifying* in the passage. One definition below is a *synonym* for that word; it means the same or almost the same thing. One definition is an *antonym*; it has the opposite or nearly opposite meaning. The other has a completely different meaning. Label the definitions S for *synonym*, A for *antonym*, and D for *different*.

   _____ a. preserving

   _____ b. changing

   _____ c. renewing

2. **Distinguishing Fact from Opinion**

   Two of the statements below present *facts*, which can be proved correct. The other statement is an *opinion*, which expresses someone's thoughts or beliefs. Label the statements F for *fact* and O for *opinion*.

   _____ a. Color vision depends on structures within the eye.

   _____ b. Red and green looked the same to John Dalton.

   _____ c. Dalton got other people interested in color blindness.

3. Keeping Events in Order

Label the statements below 1, 2, and 3 to show the order in which the events happened.

_____ a. Researchers discovered the kind of color blindness Dalton had.

_____ b. Dalton studied color blindness.

_____ c. John Dalton realized that he saw colors differently from other people.

4. Making Correct Inferences

Two of the statements below are correct *inferences*, or reasonable guesses. They are based on information in the passage. The other statement is an incorrect, or faulty, inference. Label the statements C for *correct* inference and F for *faulty* inference.

_____ a. Although Dalton was wrong, his work was important.

_____ b. Dalton's color blindness was rare and unusual.

_____ c. How we see colors is still an active topic for research.

5. Understanding Main Ideas

One of the statements below expresses the main idea of the passage. One statement is too general, or too broad. The other explains only part of the passage; it is too narrow. Label the statements M for *main idea,* B for *too broad,* and N for *too narrow.*

_____ a. Research on color blindness has been going on for a long time.

_____ b. To John Dalton, red and green looked alike, and pink flowers looked blue in daylight.

_____ c. John Dalton was the first person to research color blindness and how we see colors.

Correct Answers, Part A _____

Correct Answers, Part B _____

Total Correct Answers _____

Take a Deep Breath

Food is vital to humans. They have to eat because food keeps them strong and active. Yet people have been known to live without food for several weeks. Water is even more important to humans. Without it, nobody can live for more than a few days. But even more important to human bodies than food and water is the air around them. They cannot live for more than a few minutes without breathing.

Humans usually breathe from sixteen to twenty times each minute. If you analyzed the air you breathe, you would find it is a mixture of different gases. Most of it is nitrogen—about four-fifths. One-fifth is oxygen. There is also a tiny amount of carbon dioxide, a little water vapor (which gives air its humidity), and some traces of what are called rare gases.

If you were to put a bag over your nose and mouth to catch the air you breathe out, you would find some strange changes. There would still be the same amount of nitrogen. There would also be the same traces of rare gases. But there would be much less oxygen and a hundred times more carbon dioxide than in the air you breathed in. There would also be considerably more water vapor.

What happens is that each time you breathe, an exchange takes place. You keep some oxygen; you breathe out much more carbon dioxide and water vapor than you breathed in. The reason is that every moment of the day and night your body is using up energy. Your heart uses up energy as it beats. Your muscles use up energy. So does your brain, and so does every other part of you. All this energy is produced by the work of the millions and millions of cells that make up your body. Every one of these cells needs oxygen in order to do its work.

As the cells use up oxygen, they form carbon dioxide. This is a waste product, just as smoke and ashes are the waste products of a fire. The cells must get rid of this waste.

So your body carries out these two processes at the same time. You breathe in the oxygen that the cells need to produce energy. You breathe out the carbon dioxide that is harmful. It sounds so simple. Yet your life depends on these processes happening day and night without interruption.

Reading Time _____

Recalling Facts

1. No one can live for more than a few days without
   - ❏ a. breathing.
   - ❏ b. food.
   - ❏ c. water.

2. Humans usually breathe about
   - ❏ a. 18 times a minute.
   - ❏ b. 25 times a minute.
   - ❏ c. 10 times a minute.

3. Air is made up mostly of
   - ❏ a. oxygen.
   - ❏ b. carbon dioxide.
   - ❏ c. nitrogen.

4. To produce energy, cells need
   - ❏ a. carbon dioxide.
   - ❏ b. nitrogen.
   - ❏ c. oxygen.

5. A waste product of cells using oxygen is
   - ❏ a. nitrogen.
   - ❏ b. carbon dioxide.
   - ❏ c. water vapor.

Understanding Ideas

6. You can conclude from the article that the most vital element to life is
   - ❏ a. water.
   - ❏ b. food.
   - ❏ c. air.

7. It is likely that compared to a body in motion, a body at rest
   - ❏ a. uses less energy.
   - ❏ b. uses more energy.
   - ❏ c. uses energy at about the same rate.

8. You can conclude from the article that gasping for breath indicates that the body
   - ❏ a. needs more oxygen.
   - ❏ b. needs less oxygen.
   - ❏ c. is using more carbon dioxide.

9. The article suggests that rare gases
   - ❏ a. play an important role in breathing.
   - ❏ b. are probably unimportant to breathing.
   - ❏ c. are a by-product of breathing.

10. You can conclude from the article that as you breathe, the balance of gases
    - ❏ a. always stays the same.
    - ❏ b. varies according to circumstances.
    - ❏ c. depends mainly on where you are.

Is the air you breathe the same air the dinosaurs breathed? No, say some scientists. Eighty million years ago, when dinosaurs walked the Earth, air contained almost twice as much oxygen as it does today. How did scientists find this out? They analyzed bubbles of air trapped in amber.

Amber is a hard, yellow or brown material that is often used in jewelry. It was formed when the sap from pine trees was covered with soil. Over time, the pressure hardened the sap into a fossil. As the sap hardened, it trapped tiny air bubbles. Amber has been found that is millions of years old.

Two scientists, Gary Landis of the U.S. Geological Survey and Robert Berner of Yale University, came up with a way to analyze the air in amber. They placed 80-million-year-old amber in a vacuum chamber. Then they pumped all the modern air out of the chamber. Next, a machine inside the chamber crushed the amber. This released the ancient air inside the amber. Analysis of the air showed that it contained 32 percent oxygen. Our present-day atmosphere contains only 21 percent oxygen.

Scientists may use the information they gain from their studies of ancient air to explain other changes that have taken place on Earth.

1. **Recognizing Words in Context**

   Find the word *gain* in the passage. One definition below is a *synonym* for that word; it means the same or almost the same thing. One definition is an *antonym;* it has the opposite or nearly opposite meaning. The other has a completely different meaning. Label the definitions S for *synonym,* A for *antonym,* and D for *different.*

   _____ a. increase

   _____ b. lose

   _____ c. obtain

2. **Distinguishing Fact from Opinion**

   Two of the statements below present *facts,* which can be proved correct. The other statement is an *opinion,* which expresses someone's thoughts or beliefs. Label the statements F for *fact* and O for *opinion.*

   _____ a. Amber contains tiny bubbles of trapped air.

   _____ b. Dinosaurs found it easier to breathe than we do today.

   _____ c. The air contained more oxygen 80 million years ago than it does today.

3. Keeping Events in Order

Two of the statements below describe events that happened at the same time. The other statement describes an event that happened before or after those events. Label them S for *same time,* B for *before,* and A for *after.*

_____ a. The sap from pine trees hardens to form amber.

_____ b. Scientists analyze the air trapped in amber.

_____ c. Tiny bubbles of air are trapped in the sap.

4. Making Correct Inferences

Two of the statements below are correct *inferences,* or reasonable guesses. They are based on information in the passage. The other statement is an incorrect, or faulty, inference. Label the statements C for *correct* inference and F for *faulty* inference.

_____ a. Dinosaurs became extinct because there was less and less oxygen in the atmosphere.

_____ b. The decrease in oxygen in the air took place over millions of years.

_____ c. By analyzing air in amber of different ages, scientists can compare how air has changed over time.

5. Understanding Main Ideas

One of the statements below expresses the main idea of the passage. One statement is too general, or too broad. The other explains only part of the passage; it is too narrow. Label the statements M for *main idea,* B for *too broad,* and N for *too narrow.*

_____ a. Scientific study of insects, plant matter, and air trapped in amber has yielded a vast amount of information about the world long ago.

_____ b. Amber was placed inside a vacuum chamber and crushed, releasing the air trapped inside it.

_____ c. By analyzing air bubbles trapped in amber, scientists discovered that 80 million years ago the atmosphere contained almost twice as much oxygen as it does today.

Correct Answers, Part A _____

Correct Answers, Part B _____

Total Correct Answers _____

10 A Training Your Puppy

Any young dog can be trained to follow commands and do simple tricks. When correctly trained, a puppy will respond to your commands and gestures. Once you decide to train a puppy, however, you must be willing to stick with the job until the puppy learns.

First, you should select a simple name for the dog. Use the name frequently so that the puppy learns to recognize it.

A training session is best begun when the puppy is hungry because it is more alert at that time. Also, you can reward correct responses with a dog biscuit or meat tidbit. The hungry dog will learn to associate the correct performance of a task with a food reward and be more likely to repeat the task correctly again looking for another reward.

To get the puppy into a collar, entice it to you by extending your open hands. Pat it and say "good dog" when it comes. Then slip the collar around its neck. Next, attach a leash to the collar. If the puppy has confidence in you, it will walk along with you even though it is wearing the leash. A metal chain leash is often best because the puppy cannot chew and play with it.

Wait until a puppy is at least six months old before trying to teach it tricks. But do teach it the meaning of "no" at an earlier age. Formal training sessions should entail no more than ten minutes of work at a time. They should never tire the dog.

Teach the command "stay." While the dog is sitting, raise your palm toward the dog and order it to "stay." It will probably try to get up, so tell it "no." Whenever it remains in the sitting position after you have given the command, reward the dog with a tidbit.

More effort might be needed to teach the command "come." When the dog has learned to stay, command it to come and call it by name. When it comes to you, lavish the dog with praise and give it a snack. A stubborn dog might have to be pulled with a cord tied around its collar while the command is given.

If the training sessions are not going well, break them off. Resume them later in the day or even on another day. Give praise and tidbits to the dog only when they are earned.

Reading Time _____

Recalling Facts

1. The first step in training a puppy is to
   - ❏ a. feed the puppy.
   - ❏ b. name the puppy.
   - ❏ c. collar the puppy.

2. A puppy should be trained when it
   - ❏ a. is hungry.
   - ❏ b. is six months old.
   - ❏ c. has just been fed.

3. Formal training sessions should be limited to
   - ❏ a. no more than ten minutes of work at a time.
   - ❏ b. half an hour, once a week.
   - ❏ c. two times a day.

4. When a dog performs properly, it should be
   - ❏ a. allowed to rest.
   - ❏ b. rewarded with food.
   - ❏ c. commanded to sit.

5. If training sessions are not going well, a trainer should
   - ❏ a. punish the puppy.
   - ❏ b. wait until the puppy is older.
   - ❏ c. temporarily break off training.

Understanding Ideas

6. The article suggests that dogs should be taught commands
   - ❏ a. in order of difficulty.
   - ❏ b. in whatever way an owner chooses.
   - ❏ c. only in the morning.

7. Good training requires a
   - ❏ a. smart dog.
   - ❏ b. dedicated owner.
   - ❏ c. strong leash.

8. It is likely that puppies are better able to remember names that
   - ❏ a. are spoken loudly.
   - ❏ b. are short and simple.
   - ❏ c. are long and complicated.

9. You can conclude from the article that dogs learn best when they are rewarded
   - ❏ a. at the beginning of each training session.
   - ❏ b. at the end of each training session.
   - ❏ c. for performing correctly.

10. You can conclude from the article that dogs learn faster when
    - ❏ a. they have confidence in the trainer.
    - ❏ b. they are well fed.
    - ❏ c. trainers show affection.

10 | B | Rescue Dog in Training

"Good girl!" Kelly told her golden retriever, Ariel. The three-month-old puppy had just found a "lost" hiker. Kelly and Ariel were training as volunteers for Mountain Rescue Dogs. One day, Ariel might rescue a person who really was lost in the woods or buried in snow. The boy she had just found was a volunteer. Ariel and the other puppies loved playing this game of hide-and-seek. What was fun for the puppies now would become serious work someday.

When Ariel was a little older, she would be trained to find volunteers buried in the snow. To teach the dogs to uncover victims' heads first, the volunteers were buried with toys next to their heads.

Kelly led Ariel on to the next exercise, an obstacle course. As Kelly urged the puppy on, Ariel climbed a ladder and walked across a narrow plank. This game helped Ariel become surefooted and comfortable with heights. The last exercise of the day was a treat—riding a ski lift. Rescue dogs have to travel in all kinds of vehicles, including helicopters. Ariel jumped onto the moving chair and sat happily next to Kelly. "You're going to make a great rescue dog!" Kelly told her. Ariel just thumped her tail.

1. **Recognizing Words in Context**

   Find the word *exercise* in the passage. One definition below is a *synonym* for that word; it means the same or almost the same thing. One definition is an *antonym;* it has the opposite or nearly opposite meaning. The other has a completely different meaning. Label the definitions S for *synonym,* A for *antonym,* and D for *different.*

   _____ a. performance

   _____ b. drill

   _____ c. rest

2. **Distinguishing Fact from Opinion**

   Two of the statements below present *facts,* which can be proved correct. The other statement is an *opinion,* which expresses someone's thoughts or beliefs. Label the statements F for *fact* and O for *opinion.*

   _____ a. Ariel was going to be a great rescue dog.

   _____ b. Ariel was a three-month-old golden retriever puppy.

   _____ c. Ariel and Kelly were training to become volunteers with Mountain Rescue Dogs.

3. Keeping Events in Order

Label the statements below 1, 2, and 3 to show the order in which the events happened.

_____ a. "Good girl!" Kelly told Ariel.

_____ b. A volunteer hid in the woods, pretending to be lost.

_____ c. Ariel found the "lost" person.

4. Making Correct Inferences

Two of the statements below are correct *inferences*, or reasonable guesses. They are based on information in the passage. The other statement is an incorrect, or faulty, inference. Label the statements C for *correct* inference and F for *faulty* inference.

_____ a. The training was made into a game for the puppies.

_____ b. Only golden retrievers can become rescue dogs.

_____ c. To become a rescue dog, a puppy must learn many different skills.

5. Understanding Main Ideas

One of the statements below expresses the main idea of the passage. One statement is too general, or too broad. The other explains only part of the passage; it is too narrow. Label the statements M for *main idea*, B for *too broad*, and N for *too narrow*.

_____ a. Before becoming rescue dogs, puppies receive training in a variety of skills.

_____ b. Dogs serve humans in many different ways.

_____ c. Volunteers were buried in the snow with toys next to their heads.

Correct Answers, Part A _____

Correct Answers, Part B _____

Total Correct Answers _____

11   A   Building the Pyramids

The pyramids and other tombs were built on the west bank of the Nile River. The Egyptians chose the west bank as the "land of the dead" because that was where the dying sun disappeared each evening.

The building of the pyramids was generally started during the dry season of May and June. That was when the Nile River was at its lowest level. The crops of the year before had been harvested. The ground was now dry and cracked under a baking sun. The farmers had no work to do in the fields.

The farmers became pyramid builders. They were paid for their labor in food and clothing. The workers were provided with tools. There were no coins or other types of money used in Egypt at that time. Many of the farmers probably worked on the pyramids of their own free will rather than as forced labor. The work was a means of adding to their livelihood.

Once the Nile flood began, barges were able to bring stones down the river from the distant quarries. The stones could be unloaded close to the building sites at the desert's edge. But most of the stone used in the pyramids came from the surrounding desert itself. On land, the stones were transported on sleds with wide wooden runners. Wheels would probably have been useless. They would have sunk at once into the sand.

Every step of the work was accomplished with human labor. The huge blocks of stone were cut and shaped by hand. Tools of flint or copper were used. The Egyptians had no iron. The stones were lifted and hauled onto the sleds with the help of wooden wedges. Stout wooden bars were used as levers. The sleds themselves were not pulled by animals but by teams of men. The oxen and donkeys that the Egyptians used for fieldwork could not have been fed and watered in the harsh desert.

As the pyramid grew taller, the blocks of stone were pulled uphill on ramps made of rocks, sand, and mud. Logs, laid crosswise on the ramps, were embedded in the mud every few feet. They acted as stoppers to keep the heavy loads from slipping backward. Any interior rooms or passages had to be finished before the upper part of the pyramid was completed.

Altogether about eighty pyramids were built as burying places for the kings of Egypt.

Reading Time _____

Recalling Facts

1. Pyramids were built as
   - ❏ a. houses for the wealthy.
   - ❏ b. burial places.
   - ❏ c. warehouses.

2. Pyramids were built on the west bank of the Nile because
   - ❏ a. the ground was softer there.
   - ❏ b. the sun rose in that direction.
   - ❏ c. the sun set in that direction.

3. For building the pyramids, farmers received
   - ❏ a. high wages.
   - ❏ b. food and clothing.
   - ❏ c. gold.

4. Stones from the desert were brought to the building site
   - ❏ a. on wheeled carts.
   - ❏ b. on sleds with wide wooden runners.
   - ❏ c. by boat.

5. Tools used to build the pyramids were made of
   - ❏ a. iron.
   - ❏ b. strong wood.
   - ❏ c. flint or copper.

Understanding Ideas

6. Farmers worked on the pyramids when the Nile River was low, which suggests that the river
   - ❏ a. provided water for growing crops.
   - ❏ b. frequently dried up.
   - ❏ c. was the only source of water in Egypt.

7. You can conclude from the article that building a pyramid
   - ❏ a. was a year-round job.
   - ❏ b. was done solely by farmers.
   - ❏ c. took many years.

8. According to the article, the Egyptians were
   - ❏ a. clever engineers.
   - ❏ b. good farmers.
   - ❏ c. talented artists.

9. The article suggests that building the pyramids was
   - ❏ a. very difficult.
   - ❏ b. easy work.
   - ❏ c. wasteful.

10. You can conclude from the article that Egyptian kings wanted
    - ❏ a. small, simple tombs.
    - ❏ b. to be forgotten after they died.
    - ❏ c. to be remembered after they died.

When the Egyptian pharaoh Khufu died in 2567 B.C., his body was treated with chemicals to preserve it. Then it was wrapped in bandages. After many rituals, the pharaoh's body was brought to the Great Pyramid at Giza that would be his tomb.

Priests carried the pharaoh's wooden coffin up a low, narrow passageway to the burial chamber. There it was placed in a stone outer coffin. Surrounding the coffin was everything the pharaoh would need in the next life.

The priests performed the final ceremonies. Then workers began to seal the tomb to prevent grave robbers from stealing the pharaoh's possessions. First, they knocked away props holding up three large stone gratings at the chamber's entrance. These slid down, blocking the doorway. Three more huge blocks of stone blocked the narrow passageway. The priests and workers left through a shaft. They blocked the entrance to the shaft with a stone slab. Finally, a stone door closed off the only entrance into the pyramid. This door was then hidden behind casing stone.

All of these precautions failed to stop grave robbers, though. When European explorers entered the tomb in the sixteenth century, all they found was the pharaoh's empty stone coffin.

1. **Recognizing Words in Context**

Find the word *seal* in the passage. One definition below is a *synonym* for that word; it means the same or almost the same thing. One definition is an *antonym;* it has the opposite or nearly opposite meaning. The other has a completely different meaning. Label the definitions S for *synonym,* A for *antonym,* and D for *different.*

_____ a. open

_____ b. secure

_____ c. sea animal

2. **Distinguishing Fact from Opinion**

Two of the statements below present *facts,* which can be proved correct. The other statement is an *opinion,* which expresses someone's thoughts or beliefs. Label the statements F for *fact* and O for *opinion.*

_____ a. The grave robbers were smarter than the people who designed and built the tomb.

_____ b. The pharaoh's body was treated with chemicals to preserve it.

_____ c. The wooden coffin was placed in a large stone coffin.

3. Keeping Events in Order

Label the statements below 1, 2, and 3 to show the order in which the events happened.

_____ a. Large stone gratings slid down to block the entrance to the burial chamber.

_____ b. A stone door closed off the only entrance to the tomb.

_____ c. Three blocks of stone blocked the narrow passageway.

4. Making Correct Inferences

Two of the statements below are correct *inferences*, or reasonable guesses. They are based on information in the passage. The other statement is an incorrect, or faulty, inference. Label the statements C for *correct* inference and F for *faulty* inference.

_____ a. Only the priests and workers knew how to get into the burial chamber.

_____ b. The Egyptians believed in an afterlife.

_____ c. Special care was taken with the final resting place of a pharaoh.

5. Understanding Main Ideas

One of the statements below expresses the main idea of the passage. One statement is too general, or too broad. The other explains only part of the passage; it is too narrow. Label the statements M for *main idea*, B for *too broad*, and N for *too narrow*.

_____ a. Despite steps taken to prevent grave robbers from entering the tomb of the pharaoh Khufu, European explorers found the tomb empty.

_____ b. A stone door closed off the only entrance into the pyramid.

_____ c. For more than 4,000 years, the Pyramids of Giza have been regarded as one of the wonders of the world.

Correct Answers, Part A _____

Correct Answers, Part B _____

Total Correct Answers _____

Crabs

Crabs have flatter, broader bodies than do lobsters, crayfish, and shrimp. Their front legs have large pinching claws. In crabs that swim, the last pair of legs are broad and flattened, serving as paddles. Crabs' eyes are mounted on movable stalks. Crabs that live in water breathe by means of gills. Land crabs have modified gills that function as lungs. Some crabs feed on vegetable matter. Others eat small living animals. Most crabs, however, are scavengers, eating dead or decaying material.

Many different kinds of crabs live throughout the world. Most crabs live in the sea, on or near the bottom. Some crabs live on land, sometimes several miles from water. To lay their eggs, the females must return to the water. Ghost crabs stay on the ocean shore above the high-water line. Fiddler crabs are common along the Atlantic coast in areas of salt and brackish water. The male fiddler has an enlarged right claw that it waves back and forth as a signal to available females and to competing males. Fiddlers live in burrows in the sand or mud, where they stay during winter and high tides.

Most hermit crabs have long, soft abdomens that are spirally coiled. They occupy abandoned snail shells by thrusting the abdomen into the shell and holding onto it. They do not kill the original owner of the shell, though. They will fight other hermit crabs to determine occupancy of a shell. The hermit crab drags the shell behind as it walks about. When the crab grows larger, it seeks a larger shell.

A common crab along the Atlantic and Gulf coasts of the United States is the blue crab. Blue crabs are swimming crabs that live in marine waters but also enter shallow brackish areas.

Crabs are an important food source. Some are canned and others are sold fresh to restaurants. In the United States, three main kinds of crabs are caught for their meat. Blue crabs are caught commercially in open water by trawls or are removed from the mud with dredges. Dungeness crabs are native to the Pacific coastlines of North America. King crabs, the largest crabs, come from the North Pacific and the Bering Sea. A single king crab can provide as much as 5 pounds (2.3 kilograms) of meat. Various kinds of stone, rock, and sand crabs are gathered along coasts for food, but they are not commercially important.

Reading Time _____

Recalling Facts

1. A crab's front legs
   - ❏ a. serve as paddles.
   - ❏ b. have large pinching claws.
   - ❏ c. have gills.

2. Crabs that live in water breathe by means of
   - ❏ a. lungs.
   - ❏ b. gills.
   - ❏ c. modified gills.

3. Most crabs live
   - ❏ a. on land.
   - ❏ b. in rivers and streams.
   - ❏ c. in the sea.

4. The largest crabs are called
   - ❏ a. blue crabs.
   - ❏ b. king crabs.
   - ❏ c. dinosaur crabs.

5. Fiddler crabs live in
   - ❏ a. deep water.
   - ❏ b. snail shells.
   - ❏ c. sand or mud.

Understanding Ideas

6. Swimming crabs have broad, flattened rear legs, which
   - ❏ a. help them swim more efficiently.
   - ❏ b. help them breathe.
   - ❏ c. aid in jumping.

7. A crab's large, pinching claws would likely be useful for
   - ❏ a. walking.
   - ❏ b. capturing food.
   - ❏ c. breathing.

8. You can conclude from the article that a hermit crab lives in an empty snail shell
   - ❏ a. to protect its long, soft abdomen.
   - ❏ b. because it feeds on snails.
   - ❏ c. to deposit eggs.

9. Fiddler crabs probably got their name from
   - ❏ a. where they live.
   - ❏ b. the sound they make while burrowing.
   - ❏ c. their habit of waving their large right claw.

10. It is likely that the differences among crabs are a result of
    - ❏ a. their need to adapt to their environment.
    - ❏ b. their choice of food.
    - ❏ c. different fishing techniques.

12 B   The Most Ancient Crab

Horseshoe crabs are one of the world's oldest creatures. Scientists believe they lived in the time of the dinosaurs. But now these crabs may be in danger. Each spring they come into shore on the high tide to lay their eggs. At the same time, thousands of sea birds arrive to feast on the crab eggs. Many of these birds have flown thousands of miles, and the rich crab eggs nourish them and give them strength. There have always been plenty of eggs for both new crabs to be born and birds to eat.

Now, however, there are fewer crabs making the journey to land. Horseshoe crabs make good fishing bait. Fishers come to the shores and scoop up the female crabs before they can lay their eggs. The fishing business may be taking as many as two million crabs each year from eastern shores.

Naturalists worry that the number of crabs is dwindling. Five years ago, the crabs on one beach numbered in the millions; now the count is down to about 200,000. Naturalists also worry that the migrating birds will disappear if there are not enough crab eggs for them to eat. The fishers say they need the bait and there are plenty of crabs. For now, both sides can only watch and wait.

1. **Recognizing Words in Context**

   Find the word *dwindling* in the passage. One definition below is a *synonym* for that word; it means the same or almost the same thing. One definition is an *antonym*; it has the opposite or nearly opposite meaning. The other has a completely different meaning. Label the definitions S for *synonym*, A for *antonym*, and D for *different*.

   _____ a. growing

   _____ b. lessening

   _____ c. appearing

2. **Distinguishing Fact from Opinion**

   Two of the statements below present *facts*, which can be proved correct. The other statement is an *opinion*, which expresses someone's thoughts or beliefs. Label the statements F for *fact* and O for *opinion*.

   _____ a. Horseshoe crabs come to shore to lay their eggs.

   _____ b. Birds eat the crab eggs.

   _____ c. Horseshoe crabs may be in danger.

3. Keeping Events in Order

Label the statements below 1, 2, and 3 to show the order in which the events happened.

_____ a. Fishers collect female crabs.

_____ b. Horseshoe crabs come to shore to lay eggs.

_____ c. The number of crabs is dropping.

4. Making Correct Inferences

Two of the statements below are correct *inferences*, or reasonable guesses. They are based on information in the passage. The other statement is an incorrect, or faulty, inference. Label the statements C for *correct* inference and F for *faulty* inference.

_____ a. Taking crabs for bait may threaten their survival.

_____ b. Sea birds' lives depend on crab eggs.

_____ c. Having fewer crab eggs will have no effect on birds.

5. Understanding Main Ideas

One of the statements below expresses the main idea of the passage. One statement is too general, or too broad. The other explains only part of the passage; it is too narrow. Label the statements M for *main idea*, B for *too broad*, and N for *too narrow*.

_____ a. Horseshoe crabs are very old.

_____ b. On one beach alone, the number of horseshoe crabs dropped from millions to about 200,000.

_____ c. Horseshoe crabs and the sea birds that depend on the crabs' eggs may be in danger from people collecting the crabs for bait.

Correct Answers, Part A _____

Correct Answers, Part B _____

Total Correct Answers _____

13   A   Written by Hand

All through the early Middle Ages, the only books were those produced by monks. Such books were called manuscripts, which means "written by hand." Before the invention of the printing press, all books were carefully and painstakingly written by hand. The monks who made books were called scribes. All day long, except when they were praying, scribes sat in small rooms copying huge volumes with great patience and skill. In some monasteries, there was a large writing room called a scriptorium. Here all the monks who were skillful writers or illustrators worked together writing books.

There were very strict rules in the scriptorium. No one except the scribes and the head of the monastery were allowed to enter. One monk supervised the work. He had to provide all the necessary materials and give out the work to the others. No one was allowed to speak. Scribes used sign language to make known their needs.

Books in medieval days were not made of paper. Some were written on vellum, which was made from calf's skin. Others were written on parchment made from sheep's skin. The monks prepared the vellum and parchment themselves. Ink was made from soot mixed with gum and acid. Pens were fashioned from goose quills or reeds.

With everything in place, the scribe began the work of writing, slowly forming the large, square, curious-looking Gothic letters in use at that time. Day after day, month after month, the patient scribe bent over his sheets of vellum or parchment, forming each letter perfectly. Over time, the book grew larger and longer. It was often with a sense of relief that a monk finished his long task.

When all the pages were finished, they were usually bound in leather. Some books were covered with velvet, some with delicately carved ivory. Some covers were made of beaten gold and set with pearls and other jewels.

The monks copied Bibles, hymns and prayers, and the lives of saints. They also copied the writings of the Greeks and Romans and other ancient peoples. In this way, they saved the stories and histories that otherwise would have been lost to the world.

The scribes did a great service to civilization. Through their work, many valuable books are preserved for us today. Many of these beautiful books are still kept in museums and libraries, both in Europe and the United States. They are regarded as treasures.

Reading Time _____

Recalling Facts

1. Manuscripts are books
   - ❏ a. written by monks.
   - ❏ b. written by hand.
   - ❏ c. printed on presses.

2. Monks lived in
   - ❏ a. churches.
   - ❏ b. scriptoriums.
   - ❏ c. monasteries.

3. Scribes were monks who
   - ❏ a. made books.
   - ❏ b. built churches.
   - ❏ c. preached.

4. In the early Middle Ages, books were usually bound in
   - ❏ a. paper.
   - ❏ b. fabric.
   - ❏ c. leather.

5. Early pens were made from
   - ❏ a. reeds.
   - ❏ b. gum and acid.
   - ❏ c. leather.

Understanding Ideas

6. You can conclude from the article that books made by monks were mostly
   - ❏ a. works of fiction.
   - ❏ b. original works.
   - ❏ c. copied from other sources.

7. You can conclude from the article that books in medieval times were considered
   - ❏ a. commonplace.
   - ❏ b. rare and valuable.
   - ❏ c. a waste of time.

8. The article suggests that making books
   - ❏ a. was an exciting task.
   - ❏ b. was tedious work.
   - ❏ c. required little skill.

9. It is likely that after the printing press was invented, books
   - ❏ a. continued to be written by hand.
   - ❏ b. became less readable.
   - ❏ c. became more common.

10. The article suggests that without scribes,
   - ❏ a. many early writings would not have been preserved.
   - ❏ b. nothing would be known of early civilizations.
   - ❏ c. there would be no printing presses.

13 B Making Parchment

Brother Theophilus has been showing us how to make parchment. Last week we took the skin of a young goat—we could have used a sheepskin as well—and washed it. Then we put it to soak in limewater. After several days, we took the skin out, scraped away the hair, and returned the skin to fresh limewater. Then we took the skin out again, washed it, and stretched it on a frame to dry.

Theophilus demonstrated how to shave the skin to the right thickness. Twice more we wet the skin and put it in the sun to dry. Each time we rubbed powdered pumice into it to smooth the surface. We tightened the frame to make sure the skin was stretching evenly. The sun bleached the skin white and made it become more opaque. We will be able to write on both sides of the parchment without the ink showing through.

Before we use this parchment, we will rub it with alum to harden the surface. Then the ink will stay fresh and bright. After all, copying a book is hard work. We do not want the ink to fade. Theophilus oversees every aspect of parchment making so that our books will last forever.

1. **Recognizing Words in Context**

   Find the word *stretched* in the passage. One definition below is a *synonym* for that word; it means the same or almost the same thing. One definition is an *antonym;* it has the opposite or nearly opposite meaning. The other has a completely different meaning. Label the definitions S for *synonym*, A for *antonym*, and D for *different*.

   _____ a. reached

   _____ b. enlarged

   _____ c. shrank

2. **Distinguishing Fact from Opinion**

   Two of the statements below present *facts*, which can be proved correct. The other statement is an *opinion*, which expresses someone's thoughts or beliefs. Label the statements F for *fact* and O for *opinion*.

   _____ a. The goatskin was soaked in limewater.

   _____ b. Copying a book is hard work.

   _____ c. Parchment can be made of goatskin or sheepskin.

3. Keeping Events in Order

Two of the statements below describe events that happened at the same time. The other statement describes an event that happened before or after those events. Label them S for *same time,* B for *before,* and A for *after.*

_____ a. The goatskin becomes opaque.

_____ b. Hair is scraped off the skin.

_____ c. The sun bleaches the goatskin.

4. Making Correct Inferences

Two of the statements below are correct *inferences,* or reasonable guesses. They are based on information in the passage. The other statement is an incorrect, or faulty, inference. Label the statements C for *correct* inference and F for *faulty* inference.

_____ a. The narrator is a student of Brother Theophilus.

_____ b. The events in the passage happened long ago.

_____ c. Parchment and paper are made in the same way.

5. Understanding Main Ideas

One of the statements below expresses the main idea of the passage. One statement is too general, or too broad. The other explains only part of the passage; it is too narrow. Label the statements M for *main idea,* B for *too broad,* and N for *too narrow.*

_____ a. To make parchment for books, monks soaked, washed, stretched, and dried the skin of a goat or a sheep.

_____ b. Books in medieval days were made of parchment or vellum, not paper.

_____ c. Before the parchment was used, it was rubbed with alum to keep the ink bright and fresh.

Correct Answers, Part A _____

Correct Answers, Part B _____

Total Correct Answers _____

The National Anthem

The words of the American national anthem, "The Star-Spangled Banner," were written on the spur of the moment. It was a moment when feelings were most intense. It was a moment during the War of 1812, on the night of September 13, 1814.

The British had captured an American doctor and were holding him on their fleet anchored off Baltimore, Maryland. Francis Scott Key, a young lawyer, arranged to go out under a flag of truce and ask for the doctor's release. But the British were planning an attack on Fort McHenry before moving on to attack Baltimore. They detained Key for several days until their attack would be over. Therefore, Key was himself a prisoner on the night of September 13, when he watched the beginning of the British bombardment.

The ship Key was on was anchored where he could not avoid seeing the fight. The Americans had recently suffered losses. The capitol in Washington had been burned by the enemy. The British were confident they would succeed in their new attack. They believed Key would witness his nation's defeat and destruction. It was a terrible night for him. He paced the decks, unable to sleep. He peered through the darkness trying to see the shells landing on the fort. In the twilight, just before darkness fell, he had seen a great flag of stars and stripes flying in the breeze above the fort. Would he see that same flag flying in the morning?

Gradually, the darkness began to lift. Streaks of daylight appeared in the east. There was a mist above the water and Key could not see the fort. The bombs and firing had ceased suddenly in the night. If only he could see which flag was flying!

A breeze began to blow the mist away. Straining his eyes, Key saw what he had hardly dared to hope for. With a corner shot away and one star gone, the star-spangled banner was still flying above the fort. Key was so excited that he snatched an envelope out of his pocket and began writing down the words that came to him. That very night the words were sung in a tavern in Baltimore. They were sung to an English tune that was popular at the time. The words and the tune were stirring. Patriotism was in the air. In time, the song became the American national anthem.

Reading Time _____

Recalling Facts

1. "The Star-Spangled Banner" was written during
   - ❏ a. the Civil War.
   - ❏ b. the War of 1812.
   - ❏ c. World War I.

2. Francis Scott Key was a
   - ❏ a. doctor.
   - ❏ b. teacher.
   - ❏ c. lawyer.

3. Francis Scott Key was held prisoner while the
   - ❏ a. British attacked Fort McHenry.
   - ❏ b. Americans attacked the British fleet.
   - ❏ c. capitol in Washington was burned by the enemy.

4. Key's mission was to
   - ❏ a. convince the British to surrender.
   - ❏ b. ask for the release of a prisoner.
   - ❏ c. join the British cause.

5. The music to "The Star-Spangled Banner"
   - ❏ a. was written after the words.
   - ❏ b. was written by Francis Scott Key.
   - ❏ c. was a popular English tune.

Understanding Ideas

6. As Key watched the bombardment, he probably expected
   - ❏ a. America's defeat.
   - ❏ b. Great Britain's defeat.
   - ❏ c. a truce.

7. On the night of the bombardment, Key felt
   - ❏ a. worried and afraid.
   - ❏ b. happy and content.
   - ❏ c. unconcerned.

8. Events on the night of September 13, 1814, showed that
   - ❏ a. the Americans were poor fighters.
   - ❏ b. the British were overconfident.
   - ❏ c. an attack on Baltimore could be expected.

9. You can conclude from the article that "The Star-Spangled Banner"
   - ❏ a. is poorly written.
   - ❏ b. took a long time to write.
   - ❏ c. was written very quickly.

10. The article suggests that people found the words to the national anthem
    - ❏ a. inspirational.
    - ❏ b. unexciting.
    - ❏ c. hard to sing.

To get sailors to serve on their ships, the British often seized American ships and sailors. This was one of the causes of the War of 1812. American sailors tried many tricks to escape being impressed into the British navy.

One story tells about an American fisher named Barney Beal. Barney was out on the ocean with his crew when a British man-of-war spotted their boat and sailed toward it. The British captain ordered Barney and his crew to surrender and come aboard. Barney just ignored the order. He told his workers to continue hauling in the seine net. While fish flopped onto the deck, the British captain sent a boat with twelve armed sailors to capture the fishers. Barney whispered a few words to his crew, and they kept working. Barney acted as if he hadn't even noticed the British.

Suddenly, when the British were almost upon them, Barney gave a signal. He and his crew grabbed the edge of the empty seine net and threw it over the British boat! They pulled in the net's strings, and it closed around the sailors, boat and all, trapping them. Barney and his men rowed back to shore, dragging their "catch" behind them!

1. **Recognizing Words in Context**

Find the word *impressed* in the passage. One definition below is a *synonym* for that word; it means the same or almost the same thing. One definition is an *antonym;* it has the opposite or nearly opposite meaning. The other has a completely different meaning. Label the definitions S for *synonym*, A for *antonym*, and D for *different*.

_____ a. seized

_____ b. affected

_____ c. freed

2. **Distinguishing Fact from Opinion**

Two of the statements below present *facts*, which can be proved correct. The other statement is an *opinion*, which expresses someone's thoughts or beliefs. Label the statements F for *fact* and O for *opinion*.

_____ a. The British seized American sailors to crew British ships.

_____ b. Seizing American sailors was unfair and wrong.

_____ c. British seizure of American sailors was one of the causes of the War of 1812.

3. Keeping Events in Order

Two of the statements below describe events that happened at the same time. The other statement describes an event that happened before or after those events. Label them S for *same time*, B for *before*, and A for *after*.

_____ a. The British captain ordered Barney and his crew to come aboard the man-of-war.

_____ b. Fish flopped out of the net onto the deck.

_____ c. The British captain sent a boat with armed sailors to seize Barney and his crew.

4. Making Correct Inferences

Two of the statements below are correct *inferences*, or reasonable guesses. They are based on information in the passage. The other statement is an incorrect, or faulty, inference. Label the statements C for *correct* inference and F for *faulty* inference.

_____ a. The British had been seizing American ships and sailors before 1812.

_____ b. The man-of-war was too big to sail to shore after Barney's fishing boat.

_____ c. Americans resented the capture of their sailors by the British enough to go to war.

5. Understanding Main Ideas

One of the statements below expresses the main idea of the passage. One statement is too general, or too broad. The other explains only part of the passage; it is too narrow. Label the statements M for *main idea*, B for *too broad*, and N for *too narrow*.

_____ a. The captain of a British man-of-war ordered Barney Beal and his crew to surrender and come on board.

_____ b. One of the causes of the War of 1812 was the seizure of American ships and sailors by the British.

_____ c. An American fisher named Barney Beal avoided capture by the British by throwing a fishing net over the boat of the sailors sent to seize him and his crew.

Correct Answers, Part A _____

Correct Answers, Part B _____

Total Correct Answers _____

The Cowpuncher's Partner

In the life of the western plains, cowhands, or cowpunchers, as they preferred to call themselves, stood out as the most important figures. The people themselves, the clothes they wore, and the horses they rode were all outgrowths of life on the range. The whole job of driving, roping, and handling cattle required expert riding skills.

The most important possession of all cowpunchers, their partner in every detail of their work, was their horse. It was a tough wiry animal called a bronco. It was descended perhaps from the horses brought into the Southwest by the Spaniards. The bronco was born out on the range and ran wild until it was 2 or 3 years old. Then the horse was rounded up and driven into the ranch corral. There its training as a cow horse began.

The horse was first taught never to "run on a rope." Then it learned how to lead. That means to follow at the pull of rope or rein, instead of holding back. Next, the bronco was saddled and allowed to wear itself out in the hopeless effort to throw off the saddle.

After a few days of such schooling, a bitless bridle was slipped on the horse's head. A blindfold was passed over its eyes, and the broncobuster got into the saddle. As soon as the blindfold was removed, the bronco would usually rear and try to throw its rider.

To hold that job, broncobusters had to be able to stay with the majority of their mounts on this first ride. A horse that started out with the impression that it was easy to throw a person might turn into an outlaw, useless for serious work. When the half-broken horse learned to take a bit without hurting its mouth, it was turned over to the cowpunchers. They taught the bronco the finishing touches that would make it a good cow horse.

The cowpuncher's saddle was heavy. It sometimes weighed 40 pounds (18 kilograms) or more. A broad cinch, or girth of woven cord, went under the horse's belly. Sometimes, especially when heavy roping had to be done, a second cinch was used. In front of the wide, deep saddle seat was a horn. Around it the cowpuncher took turns with a rope when bringing down a steer. The rider sat straight-legged, feet flat in the stirrups. Sometimes these stirrups were protected by heavy leather hoods.

Reading Time _____

Recalling Facts

1. Early cowhands preferred to call themselves
   - ❏ a. riders.
   - ❏ b. cowpunchers.
   - ❏ c. cowpokes.

2. Cowpunchers' valued partner was their
   - ❏ a. saddle.
   - ❏ b. rope.
   - ❏ c. bronco.

3. Broncos were trained
   - ❏ a. right after birth.
   - ❏ b. when they were 2 or 3 years old.
   - ❏ c. after being blindfolded.

4. The front of a cowpuncher's saddle was shaped like a
   - ❏ a. pie.
   - ❏ b. horn.
   - ❏ c. box.

5. The part of the saddle holding a rider's feet is called
   - ❏ a. stirrups.
   - ❏ b. cinches.
   - ❏ c. reins.

Understanding Ideas

6. A good broncobuster would have to be
   - ❏ a. an excellent rider.
   - ❏ b. a cowhand.
   - ❏ c. light in weight.

7. Broncos were trained mainly
   - ❏ a. to compete in rodeos.
   - ❏ b. for work.
   - ❏ c. as a means of transportation.

8. Broncos were used as cow horses probably because
   - ❏ a. they had to be trained.
   - ❏ b. they were easy to round up.
   - ❏ c. they were tough and wiry.

9. A half-broken horse was one that
   - ❏ a. had a broken leg.
   - ❏ b. was partially trained.
   - ❏ c. would become an outlaw.

10. You can conclude from the article that cattle raising was
   - ❏ a. important to the livelihood of early westerners.
   - ❏ b. mainly an eastern tradition.
   - ❏ c. rare in the early West.

A Trusty Partner

We had just crossed the Pecos with a herd of cattle and settled in for the night. It had been raining steadily all day. Suddenly, a bolt of lightning struck at the edge of the herd. With a roar like thunder, all twenty-five hundred head of cattle stampeded into the dark.

We were on our horses and after the cattle in moments. I rode as fast as I could, matching strides with the leaders of the stampede. I kept shooting my six-gun in front of their noses, trying to turn the herd. I trusted my horse, Nell, to keep her feet. Try as we might, though, we couldn't stop the cattle. They ran for miles, splitting up and taking off in different directions. When at last I gave up, I had no idea where I was. I knew every hand on the drive was out trying to turn the cattle. Where the other cowpunchers were and where the wagon was, I had no idea.

All I could do was trust my horse. I gave Nell her head and sat back in my saddle. We traveled for hours. I never heard a sound nor saw a sign of another horse or person. Then suddenly Nell neighed. Not far off, another horse answered her. Nell had brought me home.

1. **Recognizing Words in Context**

   Find the word *matching* in the passage. One definition below is a *synonym* for that word; it means the same or almost the same thing. One definition is an *antonym;* it has the opposite or nearly opposite meaning. The other has a completely different meaning. Label the definitions S for *synonym,* A for *antonym,* and D for *different.*

   _____ a. contrasting

   _____ b. copying

   _____ c. fighting

2. **Distinguishing Fact from Opinion**

   Two of the statements below present *facts,* which can be proved correct. The other statement is an *opinion,* which expresses someone's thoughts or beliefs. Label the statements F for *fact* and O for *opinion.*

   _____ a. A bolt of lightning stampeded the cattle.

   _____ b. The cowpuncher was lost.

   _____ c. Nell was a very smart horse.

3. Keeping Events in Order

Two of the statements below describe events that happened at the same time. The other statement describes an event that happened before or after those events. Label them S for *same time,* B for *before,* and A for *after.*

_____ a. The cowpunchers and the cattle settled in for the night.

_____ b. The narrator kept shooting his six-gun.

_____ c. The narrator matched strides with the stampede's leaders.

4. Making Correct Inferences

Two of the statements below are correct *inferences,* or reasonable guesses. They are based on information in the passage. The other statement is an incorrect, or faulty, inference. Label the statements C for *correct* inference and F for *faulty* inference.

_____ a. Cowpunchers place a great deal of trust in their horses.

_____ b. Horses never get lost.

_____ c. Cattle are afraid of lightning.

5. Understanding Main Ideas

One of the statements below expresses the main idea of the passage. One statement is too general, or too broad. The other explains only part of the passage; it is too narrow. Label the statements M for *main idea,* B for *too broad,* and N for *too narrow.*

_____ a. When a cowpuncher became lost following a cattle stampede, his horse brought him home.

_____ b. On long cattle drives, cowpunchers faced many dangers.

_____ c. A lightning bolt stampeded the herd of cattle.

Correct Answers, Part A _____

Correct Answers, Part B _____

Total Correct Answers _____

Alfred the Great

The course of English history would have been very different had it not been for King Alfred. He won renown as both a political leader and a warrior. He is justly called the Great. The England of Alfred's time was made up of four small Saxon kingdoms. The strongest was Wessex, in the south. Born in about 848, Alfred was the youngest son of the king of Wessex. Each of Alfred's three older brothers, in turn, ruled the kingdom. Alfred was by temperament a scholar. His health was never robust.

Nevertheless, in his early youth Alfred fought with his brother Ethelred against Danish invaders. Alfred was 23 when Ethelred died, but he had already won the confidence of the army. He was at once proclaimed king. By this time, the Danes had penetrated to all parts of the island. One after the other, three of the Saxon kingdoms had fallen to the Danish invaders. Under Alfred's leadership, the Saxons again found courage. The worst crisis came in the winter of 877, when the Danish king invaded Wessex with his army. In 878, Alfred was defeated at Chippenham. He was forced to go into hiding.

A few months later, Alfred forced a Danish surrender at Chippenham. The Danes agreed to a boundary between Alfred's kingdom and the Danish lands to the north. The treaty, however, did not ensure permanent peace. The Danes attacked London and the coastal towns repeatedly. In about 896, they finally admitted defeat. They stopped trying to gain a foothold in southern England.

Alfred was much more than the defender of his country. He took a keen interest in law and order. He was concerned with improving the cultural standards of his people. He encouraged industries of all kinds. He rebuilt London, which had been partly destroyed by the Danes. He collected and revised the old laws of the kingdom. He invited learned men from other countries to instruct the people. The "books most necessary for all men to know" were translated from Latin into English so that the people might read them. Alfred himself took a part in preparing the translations.

Alfred died at the age of about 51 in 899. He was not a true king of England, for he ruled less than half of the island. After his death, however, his capable son, Edward the Elder, and his grandsons extended their rule over all of England.

Reading Time _____

Recalling Facts

1. During Alfred's time, England
   - ❏ a. was Europe's leading nation.
   - ❏ b. consisted of four small kingdoms.
   - ❏ c. was never invaded.

2. Alfred fought against
   - ❏ a. Saxon kings.
   - ❏ b. German traders.
   - ❏ c. Danish invaders.

3. Alfred was forced to go into hiding
   - ❏ a. after a military defeat.
   - ❏ b. to recover his health.
   - ❏ c. when his brother died.

4. Alfred was known as a warrior and a
   - ❏ a. businessperson.
   - ❏ b. scientist.
   - ❏ c. political leader.

5. After Alfred's death, England was
   - ❏ a. ruled by his son.
   - ❏ b. divided up again.
   - ❏ c. overrun by the Danes.

Understanding Ideas

6. According to the article, Alfred was
   - ❏ a. physically strong but not too intelligent.
   - ❏ b. an admirable leader of his people.
   - ❏ c. a true king of England.

7. Alfred cannot be compared to the kings who followed him because he
   - ❏ a. did not rule the whole country.
   - ❏ b. was never really proclaimed king.
   - ❏ c. was more a warrior than a king.

8. It is likely that without Alfred's leadership,
   - ❏ a. the Saxons would have been defeated by the Danes.
   - ❏ b. the Saxons would have defeated the Danes.
   - ❏ c. the English language would have disappeared.

9. A word that might be used to describe Alfred is
   - ❏ a. deceptive.
   - ❏ b. temperamental.
   - ❏ c. dynamic.

10. If Alfred were alive today, he would most likely be
    - ❏ a. a king.
    - ❏ b. a soldier.
    - ❏ c. a lawyer or a teacher.

The Vikings—fierce fighters from Norway and Denmark—swooped down on the British Isles like a pack of wolves. One of the first reported Viking attacks on England was on the island of Lindisfarne. The monks who had settled the island had chosen it for its safety. For almost 350 years, they had lived there peacefully. Then Viking raiders arrived in the year 793.

When he heard of the attack on Lindisfarne, a scholar wrote to Ethelred, king of Northumbria: "Never before has such a terror appeared in Britain as we have now suffered . . . , nor was it thought that such an inroad from the sea could be made."

A twelfth-century writer wrote about the raid: "The pagans from the northern regions came with a naval force to Britain like stinging hornets and spread on all sides like fearful wolves, robbed, tore and slaughtered not only beasts of burden, sheep and oxen, but even . . . companies of monks and nuns. And they came to the church of Lindisfarne, laid everything waste with grievous plundering . . . and seized all the treasures of the holy church. They killed some of the brothers, took some away with them in fetters, many they drove out, . . . some they drowned in the sea."

1. **Recognizing Words in Context**

   Find the word *settled* in the passage. One definition below is a *synonym* for that word; it means the same or almost the same thing. One definition is an *antonym;* it has the opposite or nearly opposite meaning. The other has a completely different meaning. Label the definitions S for *synonym,* A for *antonym,* and D for *different.*

   _____ a. left

   _____ b. agreed

   _____ c. colonized

2. **Distinguishing Fact from Opinion**

   Two of the statements below present *facts,* which can be proved correct. The other statement is an *opinion,* which expresses someone's thoughts or beliefs. Label the statements F for *fact* and O for *opinion.*

   _____ a. The Viking attack on Lindisfarne was the worst terror the people of England had ever suffered.

   _____ b. Viking raiders attacked the island of Lindisfarne in the year 793.

   _____ c. The Vikings killed both animals and people.

3. Keeping Events in Order

Label the statements below 1, 2, and 3 to show the order in which the events happened.

_____ a. Viking raiders attacked Lindisfarne.

_____ b. Monks settled on the island of Lindisfarne.

_____ c. Many monks were killed; others were driven away or carried off.

4. Making Correct Inferences

Two of the statements below are correct *inferences*, or reasonable guesses. They are based on information in the passage. The other statement is an incorrect, or faulty, inference. Label the statements C for *correct* inference and F for *faulty* inference.

_____ a. Viking attacks were directed mostly at communities of monks and nuns.

_____ b. The monks who settled Lindisfarne expected any attack to come from the land, not the sea.

_____ c. The islanders were not prepared for the Viking attack.

5. Understanding Main Ideas

One of the statements below expresses the main idea of the passage. One statement is too general, or too broad. The other explains only part of the passage; it is too narrow. Label the statements M for *main idea*, B for *too broad*, and N for *too narrow*.

_____ a. Beginning in the late eighth century, Viking raiders staged a series of attacks on the British Isles.

_____ b. One of the first reported Viking attacks on England was on the island of Lindisfarne.

_____ c. Viking raiders plundered the treasures of the church of Lindisfarne.

Correct Answers, Part A _____

Correct Answers, Part B _____

Total Correct Answers _____

76

All Europe was excited in June 1783. Two brothers, in France, had sent a large paper bag sailing upward into the air. They had filled it with hot smoke from a straw fire. To most people of that day, the soaring bag seemed a miracle. Yet within 50 years, inventors had developed most of the principles used in ballooning today.

Airships were developed from principles of ballooning. Airships, however, have engines with propellers to drive them through the air. They have rudders to steer them. Some airships have a rigid outer fabric. Others are nonrigid and are commonly called blimps. Balloons and airships are classed as lighter-than-air craft. This distinguishes them from airplanes, gliders, and helicopters, which are heavier than air. They have to keep moving and require power from an engine to stay aloft.

A balloon rises because it is filled with a gas that is lighter than air. The total weight of the gas, the balloon bag, and the load it carries must be less than the weight of the air that would occupy the same space (the displaced air). In order to rise, the balloon must be filled with hot air or gases that are lighter than air.

Hydrogen, the lightest gas, catches fire and explodes easily. Coal gas is cheaper, but it is heavier than hydrogen and burns just as easily. Helium, with 93 percent of the lifting power of hydrogen, cannot burn. Although scarce and expensive, it is the ideal balloon gas. The main supply is found in the United States. Its use is government-controlled.

When a toy balloon is blown up by mouth, it falls to the ground. This is because the weight of the rubber and the compressed air in it make it heavier than air. But if it is placed on a radiator so that the air in it becomes hot (not too hot, or it will burst), the balloon expands. It will rise and stay aloft until the air in it cools off. A toy balloon that is filled with helium will float up. It rises until it bursts.

In principle, the round passenger balloon resembles this gas-filled toy. If it is fastened to the ground, it is called a captive balloon. When it is released to drift with the wind, it is a free balloon. The up-and-down motion of a free balloon can be controlled but not its horizontal direction.

Reading Time _____

Recalling Facts

1. Airships were developed from
   - ❏ a. paper bags.
   - ❏ b. ships at sea.
   - ❏ c. principles of ballooning.

2. Airships with nonrigid outer fabric are called
   - ❏ a. balloons.
   - ❏ b. gliders.
   - ❏ c. blimps.

3. Balloons and airships are classed as
   - ❏ a. lighter-than-air craft.
   - ❏ b. heavier-than-air craft.
   - ❏ c. hydrogen craft.

4. The ideal balloon gas is
   - ❏ a. coal.
   - ❏ b. helium.
   - ❏ c. hydrogen.

5. When a toy balloon is blown up by mouth, it
   - ❏ a. rises in the air.
   - ❏ b. falls to the ground.
   - ❏ c. moves horizontally.

Understanding Ideas

6. The fact that helium cannot burn makes it
   - ❏ a. better able to lift balloons.
   - ❏ b. the safest gas for balloons.
   - ❏ c. scarce and expensive.

7. Between airships and balloons,
   - ❏ a. balloons are more dependable as passenger craft.
   - ❏ b. airships are more dependable as passenger craft.
   - ❏ c. both are equally dependable as passenger craft.

8. You can conclude from the article that hot air
   - ❏ a. weighs the same as cool air.
   - ❏ b. is heavier than cool air.
   - ❏ c. is lighter than cool air.

9. Airships and heavier-than-air craft are alike in that both
   - ❏ a. are powered by engines.
   - ❏ b. are fueled by air.
   - ❏ c. float in the air.

10. You can conclude from the article that the up-and-down motion of a free balloon can be controlled by
   - ❏ a. heating the gas within it.
   - ❏ b. a pulley system.
   - ❏ c. releasing the gas within it.

17 B   The *Hindenburg* Disaster

Built in 1936, the German airship *Hindenburg* was the first transatlantic commercial airliner. It was also the largest, most luxurious aircraft in the world. The cigar-shaped zeppelin, or dirigible, was held aloft by sixteen huge, hydrogen-filled balloons enclosed in a fabric-covered aluminum frame. In addition to twenty-five staterooms, the airship had an elegant fifty-foot-long (15-meter-long) dining room and a lounge complete with grand piano. Windows tilting downward offered breathtaking views of land and sea.

Thunderstorms had delayed the *Hindenburg*'s arrival in Lakehurst, New Jersey, on May 6, 1937. Otherwise, the three-day flight from Frankfurt, Germany, had been uneventful, as on all the other trips the ship had made across the Atlantic. News photographers on the ground clicked their camera shutters, and radio commentators spoke into their microphones. Then, as the silver ship approached its mooring mast, there was a sudden flash. A loud explosion followed as the flammable hydrogen exploded! In less than a minute, the entire airship was ablaze!

One horrified reporter shouted into his microphone, "It's burst into flames! Oh, my . . . it's burning! . . . This is one of the worst catastrophes in the world! Oh, the humanity and all the passengers." Of the ninety-seven people on board, thirty-five lost their lives. The *Hindenburg* tragedy signaled the end of lighter-than-air travel.

1. **Recognizing Words in Context**

   Find the word *elegant* in the passage. One definition below is a *synonym* for that word; it means the same or almost the same thing. One definition is an *antonym*; it has the opposite or nearly opposite meaning. The other has a completely different meaning. Label the definitions S for *synonym*, A for *antonym*, and D for *different*.

   _____ a. splendid

   _____ b. simple

   _____ c. neat

2. **Distinguishing Fact from Opinion**

   Two of the statements below present *facts*, which can be proved correct. The other statement is an *opinion*, which expresses someone's thoughts or beliefs. Label the statements F for *fact* and O for *opinion*.

   _____ a. The *Hindenburg* burst into flames on its arrival in Lakehurst, New Jersey.

   _____ b. Thirty-five people died in the fire.

   _____ c. It was the worst catastrophe in the world.

3. Keeping Events in Order

Two of the statements below describe events that happened at the same time. The other statement describes an event that happened before or after those events. Label them S for *same time,* B for *before,* and A for *after.*

_____ a. The *Hindenburg* approached its mooring mast.

_____ b. Thunderstorms delayed the ship's arrival.

_____ c. There was a sudden flash.

4. Making Correct Inferences

Two of the statements below are correct *inferences,* or reasonable guesses. They are based on information in the passage. The other statement is an incorrect, or faulty, inference. Label the statements C for *correct* inference and F for *faulty* inference.

_____ a. The use of hydrogen gas in zeppelins was a dangerous practice.

_____ b. The *Hindenburg's* designers were not aware of the danger hydrogen represented.

_____ c. The reporter thought everyone on board the airship would be killed.

5. Understanding Main Ideas

One of the statements below expresses the main idea of the passage. One statement is too general, or too broad. The other explains only part of the passage; it is too narrow. Label the statements M for *main idea,* B for *too broad,* and N for *too narrow.*

_____ a. Because of this accident, airship travel was judged to be too dangerous, and it was abandoned.

_____ b. On the evening of May 6, 1937, the zeppelin *Hindenburg* burst into flames as it arrived in Lakehurst, New Jersey.

_____ c. Of the ninety-seven people on board the *Hindenburg,* thirty-five lost their lives.

Correct Answers, Part A _____

Correct Answers, Part B _____

Total Correct Answers _____

Ages ago, the land of Egypt was very different from what it is today. Rain fell, and the sea extended far up the Nile Valley. The plateau on each side of the water was grassland. The people wandered over the plateau in search of game and fresh pastures and had no permanent home. They hunted with a crude stone hand ax and with a bow and arrow. Their arrows were made of chipped flint. Very gradually, the rains decreased and the grasslands dried up. The Nile River began to deposit silt in the valley. The animals went down to the valley. The hunters followed them and settled at the edge of the jungle that lined the river.

In the Nile Valley, the people's way of life underwent a great change. They settled down in more or less permanent homes and progressed from food gathering to food producing. They still hunted the elephant and hippopotamus and wild fowl, and they fished in the river. More and more, however, they relied for meat on the animals they bred—long-horned cattle, sheep, goats, and geese.

Early Egyptians learned that the vegetables and wild grain they gathered grew from seeds. When the Nile floodwaters drained away, they dug up the ground with a wooden hoe, scattered seeds over the wet soil, and waited for the harvest. The people raised wheat, barley, a few vegetables, and flax. From the grain they made bread. They spun and wove the flax for linen garments.

The Egyptians' first houses were round or oval, built over a hole in the ground. The walls were lumps of mud, and the roofs were matting. Later houses were rectangular, made of shaped bricks, with wooden frames for doors and windows. The people fashioned ornaments of ivory, made beads and baskets, and carved in stone the figures of people and animals. They built ships that had oars, and they carried on trade with nearby countries.

Good farmland was scarce. The desert came down close to the marshes that edged the river. To gain more land, the people filled in the marshes and built mud walls to keep out the floodwater. In time, they engaged in large-scale irrigation work, digging canals across miles of land. This work required the cooperation of many people living in different places. Leaders became necessary to plan the work and direct the workers. Because of this need, orderly government arose.

Reading Time _____

Recalling Facts

1. Early dwellers of Egypt
   - ❑ a. lived in stone houses.
   - ❑ b. had no permanent homes.
   - ❑ c. lived on the Nile.

2. Early hunters hunted with
   - ❑ a. slingshots.
   - ❑ b. rifles.
   - ❑ c. bows and arrows.

3. The first Egyptian houses were
   - ❑ a. holes in the ground.
   - ❑ b. round or oval.
   - ❑ c. rectangular.

4. Early Egyptian ships were moved by
   - ❑ a. sails.
   - ❑ b. motors.
   - ❑ c. oars.

5. Government arose as a result of
   - ❑ a. the housing industry.
   - ❑ b. a need for planning and organizing work.
   - ❑ c. increased trade.

Understanding Ideas

6. Life changed for early Egyptians mainly because of
   - ❑ a. changes in the climate.
   - ❑ b. flooding of the Nile.
   - ❑ c. enemy invasions.

7. You can conclude from the article that desert land
   - ❑ a. is good for growing certain crops.
   - ❑ b. makes poor farmland.
   - ❑ c. can never be used for farming.

8. You can conclude from the article that farming in Egypt depended on
   - ❑ a. rain.
   - ❑ b. trade with other countries.
   - ❑ c. the Nile.

9. Irrigation is a means of
   - ❑ a. supplying dry land with water.
   - ❑ b. gathering crops.
   - ❑ c. increasing transportation.

10. You can conclude from the article that civilizations are more likely to develop where
    - ❑ a. land is fertile.
    - ❑ b. wild game is plentiful.
    - ❑ c. flooding is frequent.

Egyptian Seasons

"There are three seasons," Menna told his three sons. "The first and most important season is Inundation. That is when the Nile floods the land, bringing its life-giving waters. The second season is Emergence, when the water recedes from the land, leaving behind rich, moist soil. That is when we capture the water in our ditches and plant seeds in the mud. That is the time of year that feeds all of Egypt."

"What is the third season, Father?" asked Menna's youngest son.

"Drought, my son," Menna said. "The time when the Nile's waters have gone from the land, and the land begins to dry up. That is when we harvest and thresh our crops. And then. . . ."

"Then what, Father?" another son asked.

"Then we wait—and pray—for the next Inundation. If the Nile does not flood the land, there will be no Emergence. There will be no soil to plant. There will be no food for Egypt. There will be only Drought and, in time, hunger across the land."

Menna and his sons gazed out over their fields, which were disappearing beneath the Nile's spreading waters. "This will be a good Inundation," Menna said. "Egypt will not starve this year."

1. **Recognizing Words in Context**

   Find the word *rich* in the passage. One definition below is a *synonym* for that word; it means the same or almost the same thing. One definition is an *antonym;* it has the opposite or nearly opposite meaning. The other has a completely different meaning. Label the definitions S for *synonym,* A for *antonym,* and D for *different.*

   _____ a. wealthy

   _____ b. poor

   _____ c. fertile

2. **Distinguishing Fact from Opinion**

   Two of the statements below present *facts,* which can be proved correct. The other statement is an *opinion,* which expresses someone's thoughts or beliefs. Label the statements F for *fact* and O for *opinion.*

   _____ a. There were three seasons in the Egyptian year.

   _____ b. Inundation left behind rich soil for growing crops.

   _____ c. The ancient Egyptians were too dependent on the flooding of the Nile.

3. Keeping Events in Order

Two of the statements below describe events that happened at the same time. The other statement describes an event that happened before or after those events. Label them S for *same time*, B for *before*, and A for *after*.

_____ a. During Emergence, the land rose out of the floodwaters.

_____ b. The floodwaters left behind rich, moist soil.

_____ c. The farmers planted seeds in the mud.

4. Making Correct Inferences

Two of the statements below are correct *inferences*, or reasonable guesses. They are based on information in the passage. The other statement is an incorrect, or faulty, inference. Label the statements C for *correct* inference and F for *faulty* inference.

_____ a. The ancient Egyptians had not learned how to harness the waters of the Nile.

_____ b. Without the annual flooding of the Nile, the Egyptians would starve.

_____ c. The length of the Egyptian year was different from that in other parts of the world.

5. Understanding Main Ideas

One of the statements below expresses the main idea of the passage. One statement is too general, or too broad. The other explains only part of the passage; it is too narrow. Label the statements M for *main idea*, B for *too broad*, and N for *too narrow*.

_____ a. In ancient Egypt, people depended for their lives on the Nile River.

_____ b. The three seasons of the Egyptian year—Inundation, Emergence, and Drought—were based on the annual flooding of the Nile.

_____ c. The floodwaters left behind rich, moist soil.

Correct Answers, Part A _____

Correct Answers, Part B _____

Total Correct Answers _____

84

People's Best Friend

The dog is one of the most popular pets in the world. It ordinarily remains (1) loyal to a considerate master, and because of this trait, the dog has been called a person's best friend. Class distinctions between people have no part in a dog's life. It can be a faithful companion to either rich or poor. Dogs have been domesticated for most of human history and have thus endeared themselves to many over the years. Stories have been told about brave dogs that served admirably in war or that risked their lives to save people in danger.

A dog fits easily into family life. It thrives on praise and affection. When a master tells a dog that it is good, the animal happily wags its tail. But when a master scolds a dog, it skulks away with a sheepish look and with its tail tucked between its legs. People in cities as well as those in other areas can enjoy a dog. Medium-size or small dogs are best suited for confined city living. Large dogs need considerable exercise over a large area and thrive best in the country.

When a person decides to own a dog, he or she should be prepared to care for it properly. For a dog to stay healthy, it must be correctly fed and adequately groomed. Also, its medical needs must be met. For a dog to be well-mannered, it must be properly trained. It should never be ill-treated or mishandled. Otherwise, it will bite in its own defense.

(2) The wild ancestors of all dogs were hunters. Wolves and other wild relatives of the dog still hunt in packs for their food. Dogs have retained the (3) urge to be with the pack. This is why they do not like to be left alone for long. Some breeds of dogs still retain the hunting instinct.

Dogs exist in a wide range of sizes, colors, and temperaments. Some, (4) such as the Doberman pinscher and the German shepherd, serve as alert and aggressive watchdogs. Others, such as the beagle and the cocker spaniel, are playful family pets, even though they were bred for hunting. Still others, such as the collie and the Welsh corgi, can herd farm or range animals. Each of the dogs just mentioned is a purebred. However, a (5) mongrel dog, one with many breeds in its background, can just as easily fit into family life.

Reading Time _____

Recalling Facts

1. The dog is called a person's best friend because of its
   - → a. loyalty to a master.
   - b. ability to save lives.
   - c. friendly nature.

2. The wild ancestors of dogs were
   - a. herders.
   - → b. hunters.
   - c. cave dwellers.

3. Dogs prefer
   - a. living alone.
   - → b. being with a pack.
   - c. living indoors.

4. Dogs that make good watchdogs include
   - a. beagles.
   - b. Welsh corgis.
   - → c. German shepherds.

5. A dog with many breeds in its background is called a
   - a. purebred.
   - b. range animal.
   - → c. mongrel.

Understanding Ideas

6. Dogs are popular pets because
   - → a. of their loyalty and affectionate nature.
   - b. of their great variety.
   - c. they once were hunters.

7. You can conclude from the article that the temperament of a mongrel dog is
   - a. easy to predict.
   - → b. difficult to predict.
   - c. usually aggressive.

8. A dog that is attacked will most likely
   - a. wag its tail.
   - → b. bite to defend itself.
   - c. tuck its tail between its legs.

9. Dogs that were bred for hunting
   - → a. may make good family pets.
   - b. seldom make good family pets.
   - c. are usually aggressive animals.

10. You can conclude from the article that people choose as pets those dogs that
    - → a. best suit their needs.
    - b. easily fit into family life.
    - c. make good watchdogs.

Becoming Dogs

A small band of hunters moved through the woods following a trail of blood left by a wounded deer. Following close behind the hunters was a pack of wolves. It had been a lean season. Both humans and wolves were on the verge of starvation.

Weak from loss of blood, the wounded deer tried an old trick of its kind. Out of the hunters' sight, it doubled back on its trail. Then it veered off into a thick clump of bushes. It stood there motionless as the hunters passed by, still following the trail of blood. The humans could rely only on clues they saw. When they came to the end of the trail, they halted in confusion. To them, the deer had disappeared into thin air!

The wolves, however, picked up on the deer's scent and followed it back. For lack of anything else to do, the humans followed the wolves. When the wolves came to the deer's hiding place, they flushed it into the open. The deer, held at bay by the wolves, was an easy target for the hunters' spears. To thank the wolves, the hunters shared their kill with the pack.

The wolves had just taken their first step on the long journey to becoming dogs.

1. **Recognizing Words in Context**

Find the word *passed* in the passage. One definition below is a *synonym* for that word; it means the same or almost the same thing. One definition is an *antonym*; it has the opposite or nearly opposite meaning. The other has a completely different meaning. Label the definitions S for *synonym*, A for *antonym*, and D for *different*.

_____ a. went

_____ b. threw

_____ c. stopped

2. **Distinguishing Fact from Opinion**

Two of the statements below present *facts*, which can be proved correct. The other statement is an *opinion*, which expresses someone's thoughts or beliefs. Label the statements F for *fact* and O for *opinion*.

_____ a. The wolves picked up the scent of the deer's trail.

_____ b. The wolves deserved all of the kill, not just part of it.

_____ c. The hunters shared their kill with the wolves.

3. Keeping Events in Order

Two of the statements below describe events that happened at the same time. The other statement describes an event that happened before or after those events. Label them S for *same time,* B for *before,* and A for *after.*

_____ a. The deer doubled back on its trail.

_____ b. The wolves held the deer at bay.

_____ c. The hunters killed the deer with their spears.

4. Making Correct Inferences

Two of the statements below are correct *inferences,* or reasonable guesses. They are based on information in the passage. The other statement is an incorrect, or faulty, inference. Label the statements C for *correct* inference and F for *faulty* inference.

_____ a. The wolves' sense of smell was far better than that of the humans.

_____ b. The wolves and humans were hunting together.

_____ c. The hunters were grateful to the wolves for finding the deer.

5. Understanding Main Ideas

One of the statements below expresses the main idea of the passage. One statement is too general, or too broad. The other explains only part of the passage; it is too narrow. Label the statements M for *main idea,* B for *too broad,* and N for *too narrow.*

_____ a. A pack of wolves helped a band of hunters kill a deer.

_____ b. A pack of wolves flushed a deer into the open.

_____ c. Wolves are the ancestors of dogs.

Correct Answers, Part A _____

Correct Answers, Part B _____

Total Correct Answers _____

A skilled outdoorsperson or tracker can tell what creatures have passed through an area from the marks that they have left in the snow, soft earth, mud, or sand. Anyone can make a walk outdoors more interesting by learning to "read" the tracks left by animals. Some common animal tracks include tracks of mammals, insects, snakes, and birds.

Snow can be perfect for tracking animals. In winter, animals are very active. Finding food is more difficult at this time. They must roam far and wide in search of something to eat. Fresher tracks show more detail, but smart trackers prefer to wait a night and part of a day after a fresh snowfall. This way, both daytime and nighttime feeders have had time to leave their prints.

The muddy bank of a river or the edges of a lake may have tracks left by animals that have come to the water to drink. On wet lakeshores and along the marshy shores of ponds, there may be tracks of gulls, sandpipers, and other birds. There may also be footprints of insects, crabs, turtles, and raccoons. A few feet from the sides of a sandy desert road may be the tracks of a jackrabbit, a kangaroo rat, or a kit fox. Sand dunes carry the impressions of snakes and insects as well as the tracks of birds and other animals.

A tracker can tell many things from a set of animal tracks. The size of the prints gives a clue to the size of the animal. The tracks of the front and back feet may occur in pairs or they may alternate. Some animals walk with their toes pointed inward. Tracks can reveal whether the animal was walking or running. For example, a walking deer places its hind foot directly in the print of the front foot on the same side. When a deer runs, however, its hind feet land in front of the forefoot prints. If it is running very fast, its toes may separate more than usual as its feet hit the ground.

Sometimes tracks tell a dramatic story of flight and pursuit, of capture or escape. The animal may have crouched waiting for some prey. The tracks may suddenly bunch up and then stretch out at the point where the animal spotted its prey and took off in pursuit. Following the trail may reveal whether the animal caught its prey.

Reading Time _____

Recalling Facts

1. Trackers are
   - ❏ a. creatures passing through an area.
   - ❏ b. people who read marks left by animals.
   - ❏ c. prints left by animals.

2. The size of prints left by an animal tells
   - ❏ a. the size of the animal.
   - ❏ b. when the animal passed through an area.
   - ❏ c. the animal's sex.

3. Animal tracks can reveal
   - ❏ a. an animal's thoughts.
   - ❏ b. whether an animal was running.
   - ❏ c. the color of an animal.

4. Trackers prefer to read prints
   - ❏ a. right after a snowfall.
   - ❏ b. during a snowfall.
   - ❏ c. a night and part of a day after a snowfall.

5. Animals are very active in winter because
   - ❏ a. they must roam farther in search of food.
   - ❏ b. they must move to keep warm.
   - ❏ c. cold weather makes them hungrier.

Understanding Ideas

6. The article wants you to understand that animal tracks
   - ❏ a. all look alike.
   - ❏ b. are easy to read.
   - ❏ c. are different for each animal.

7. You can conclude from the article that frozen earth
   - ❏ a. is good for tracking animals.
   - ❏ b. is the best surface for tracking animals.
   - ❏ c. makes tracking difficult.

8. Snow is perfect for tracking animals because
   - ❏ a. details are clearer on a soft surface.
   - ❏ b. animals like walking on snow.
   - ❏ c. snow melts quickly.

9. Trackers are likely to be
   - ❏ a. studious.
   - ❏ b. curious.
   - ❏ c. greedy.

10. You can conclude from the article that hunters read animal tracks in order to
    - ❏ a. locate their prey.
    - ❏ b. avoid dangerous wild animals.
    - ❏ c. predict the weather.

20　B　The Wendigo

Native Americans of the Northeast tell tales of an evil creature called Wendigo. No one could describe it, but it was greatly feared. Its victims always answered its call when they heard it.

A group of Englishmen were being led deep into moose country by a guide. The guide soon became uneasy. He kept looking over his shoulder. That night, the men heard him crying in his sleep. Suddenly, he jumped up and shouted, "My feet are burning! They are fiery wings, and I must fly!" He disappeared into the woods.

In the morning, his companions found two sets of tracks in the snow. One set was the imprint of human feet wearing moccasins. They could not tell what kind of creature had made the other set of tracks, though. They were as huge as snowshoes!

The men followed the tracks for most of the day. As they walked, they began to notice something strange. The human prints began to take the shape of the creature's! At last, the only difference was in their size.

That night, as the men sat around a campfire, they heard noises coming toward them. In the flickering light, they saw a ragged, wild-looking man with strangely shaped feet. It was their lost guide! All he could say was "Wendigo" over and over.

1. **Recognizing Words in Context**

   Find the word *strange* in the passage. One definition below is a *synonym* for that word; it means the same or almost the same thing. One definition is an *antonym;* it has the opposite or nearly opposite meaning. The other has a completely different meaning. Label the definitions S for *synonym,* A for *antonym,* and D for *different.*

   _____ a. foreign

   _____ b. familiar

   _____ c. odd

2. **Distinguishing Fact from Opinion**

   Two of the statements below present *facts,* which can be proved correct. The other statement is an *opinion,* which expresses someone's thoughts or beliefs. Label the statements F for *fact* and O for *opinion.*

   _____ a. The men's guide became uneasy.

   _____ b. The men saw two sets of tracks in the snow.

   _____ c. Wendigo had called the guide and taken him away.

3. Keeping Events in Order

Two of the statements below describe events that happened at the same time. The other statement describes an event that happened before or after those events. Label them S for *same time*, B for *before*, and A for *after*.

_____ a. The men were sitting around a campfire.

_____ b. The men followed the tracks all day.

_____ c. The men heard noises coming toward them.

4. Making Correct Inferences

Two of the statements below are correct *inferences*, or reasonable guesses. They are based on information in the passage. The other statement is an incorrect, or faulty, inference. Label the statements C for *correct* inference and F for *faulty* inference.

_____ a. The Englishmen did not believe Wendigo existed.

_____ b. The Englishmen were concerned about what had happened to the guide.

_____ c. The guide was in a state of shock caused by his experience.

5. Understanding Main Ideas

One of the statements below expresses the main idea of the passage. One statement is too general, or too broad. The other explains only part of the passage; it is too narrow. Label the statements M for *main idea*, B for *too broad*, and N for *too narrow*.

_____ a. All the guide could say was "Wendigo" over and over.

_____ b. While leading a group of Englishmen in the forest, a guide is apparently taken away by a creature called Wendigo.

_____ c. Native Americans of the Northeast tell tales of an evil creature called Wendigo.

Correct Answers, Part A _____

Correct Answers, Part B _____

Total Correct Answers _____

When Captain James Cook and his crew were exploring the coast of Australia in 1770, they saw a strange animal. At times, the creature stood upright, braced firmly on its hind legs and huge tail. It moved by great leaps. Thus, Europeans first met the gray kangaroo.

More than a hundred species of the kangaroo family live in the open spaces of Australia, New Guinea, and nearby islands. They belong to the marsupial family, which includes those animals that carry their young in pouches.

The gray kangaroo, the best-known species of the family, reaches an average weight of 145 pounds (66 kilograms) and a length of 10 feet (3 meters) from nose to tip of tail. The tail alone is about 4 feet (1 meter) long, and the strong muscles at its base make it nearly as thick as the animal's body. Its head is relatively small. The ears are large and rounded, and the mouth is small, with prominent lips. The fur is soft and woolly and, in many individuals, is grizzled. Stripes may be present on the head, back, or upper limbs.

The kangaroo's body is specially built for jumping. There are four toes on each of the two hind feet. The two inner toes are partially fused. The second toe from the outside is much stronger and longer than the others and bears the longest claw. This toe and the shorter outside toe are used in the great leaps that the kangaroo makes. The front legs are short and slender and end in five-toed, clawed paws. The paws are used like hands to handle food. Three-fourths of the animal's size and weight are in its hindquarters. It can leap along the ground at more than 30 miles (48 kilometers) an hour.

The female has a large pouch on the belly made by a fold in the furry skin. When the baby kangaroo, or joey, is born, it is only 1 inch (2.5 centimeters) long and is only partially developed. It climbs unassisted into its mother's pouch, where it completes its growth in about ten months. When the joey is about 4 months old, it is able to lean out of the sheltering pouch and nibble grass. Soon it climbs out and learns to hop around in search of food. It continues for several weeks longer to climb back into the pouch for sleep, safety, and occasional nourishment.

Reading Time _____

Recalling Facts

1. Kangaroos carry their young
   - ❏ a. on their backs.
   - ❏ b. in their mouths.
   - ❏ c. in pouches.

2. Most kangaroos live in or near
   - ❏ a. Africa.
   - ❏ b. Australia.
   - ❏ c. the Arctic.

3. The kangaroo's body is specially built for
   - ❏ a. swimming.
   - ❏ b. jumping.
   - ❏ c. climbing.

4. Most of the kangaroo's size and weight is in its
   - ❏ a. hindquarters.
   - ❏ b. head and neck.
   - ❏ c. belly.

5. After a baby kangaroo is born, it
   - ❏ a. is able to fend for itself.
   - ❏ b. rides on its mother's back.
   - ❏ c. climbs into its mother's pouch.

Understanding Ideas

6. You can conclude from the article that Captain James Cook and his crew
   - ❏ a. had never seen a kangaroo before exploring Australia.
   - ❏ b. brought kangaroos back with them to Europe.
   - ❏ c. found Australian kangaroos terrifying.

7. You can conclude from the article that kangaroos are part of the marsupial family because they
   - ❏ a. live in Australia.
   - ❏ b. are great leapers.
   - ❏ c. share characteristics with other marsupials.

8. It is likely that if left to fend for itself after birth, a joey would
   - ❏ a. not survive.
   - ❏ b. quickly learn how to survive.
   - ❏ c. never fully develop.

9. A kangaroo's ability to leap quickly probably
   - ❏ a. helps it escape from its enemies.
   - ❏ b. is a disadvantage when searching for food.
   - ❏ c. is typical of most marsupials.

10. You can conclude from the article that a kangaroo's front legs
    - ❏ a. are not as useful as the rear legs.
    - ❏ b. help it leap higher.
    - ❏ c. serve a different function from the rear legs.

21   B   A Joey Grows Up

The baby gray kangaroo, or joey, peeked out of his mother's pouch. For the last six months, he had stayed hidden inside her pouch, suckling milk. But lately, he had begun popping his head out from time to time to take a look at the world.

The joey sniffed the grass as his mother bent down to graze. Then he leaned out of the pouch and took a nibble.

Over the next few weeks, the joey grew more daring. At first, he stayed in the pouch, resting his front paws on the ground as he ate grass. Then one day he tumbled all the way out! Startled, he pulled the pouch open and dove back in headfirst.

Soon the joey was leaving the pouch regularly. He stayed out longer and longer. Whenever something frightened him, though, he dove back into the pouch.

The day came, however, when his mother would not let him into her pouch. When he tried to pull the pouch open, she pushed him away. She was pregnant. Her pouch would be needed by the new joey when it was born. Her eight-month-old joey could survive on his own now. It was time for him to leave the pouch—for good.

1. **Recognizing Words in Context**

Find the word *grew* in the passage. One definition below is a *synonym* for that word; it means the same or almost the same thing. One definition is an *antonym*; it has the opposite or nearly opposite meaning. The other has a completely different meaning. Label the definitions S for *synonym*, A for *antonym*, and D for *different*.

_____ a. ceased

_____ b. lengthened

_____ c. became

2. **Distinguishing Fact from Opinion**

Two of the statements below present *facts*, which can be proved correct. The other statement is an *opinion*, which expresses someone's thoughts or beliefs. Label the statements F for *fact* and O for *opinion*.

_____ a. The joey stayed inside his mother's pouch for six months.

_____ b. The mother kangaroo was cruel to push the joey away.

_____ c. When the joey was eight months old, his mother would not let him into her pouch.

3. **Keeping Events in Order**

Label the statements below 1, 2, and 3 to show the order in which the events happened.

_____ a. The joey tumbled out of the pouch.

_____ b. The joey hung out of his mother's pouch and nibbled grass.

_____ c. The joey stayed out of the pouch longer and longer.

4. **Making Correct Inferences**

Two of the statements below are correct *inferences*, or reasonable guesses. They are based on information in the passage. The other statement is an incorrect, or faulty, inference. Label the statements C for *correct* inference and F for *faulty* inference.

_____ a. A joey uses its mother's pouch for protection until the mother no longer lets it.

_____ b. The eight-month-old joey will die without its mother's milk.

_____ c. A pregnant kangaroo will force an older joey to live on its own.

5. **Understanding Main Ideas**

One of the statements below expresses the main idea of the passage. One statement is too general, or too broad. The other explains only part of the passage; it is too narrow. Label the statements M for *main idea*, B for *too broad*, and N for *too narrow*.

_____ a. Kangaroos belong to the marsupial family, which includes animals that carry their young in pouches.

_____ b. A growing joey continues to use his mother's pouch for protection until he is able to survive on his own.

_____ c. For six months, the joey stayed hidden inside his mother's pouch, suckling milk.

Correct Answers, Part A _____

Correct Answers, Part B _____

Total Correct Answers _____

King Me!

Checkers is a board game of ancient origin. Each of two players tries to capture or immobilize the other's pieces. People throughout the world play variations of the game. Checkers is called draughts in Great Britain. Checkers is a war game with offensive and defensive play. Its basic principles are easy, but it can be very intricate. Checkers and chess have similar roots, but checkers is simpler and probably developed earlier. The game was played in Egypt during the time of the pharaohs, and it appears in the ancient Greek writings of Homer and Plato.

Checkers as played in the United States and Britain is the most widely played modern version. In this version, each player starts with 12 pieces called men, or checkers. A conventional checkers board consists of 64 two-inch squares in eight rows of eight squares each. The squares are colored alternately light and dark. Play is confined to one of these colors, usually the darker. The flat, round men, regardless of their actual colors, are called red and black.

The player with the black checkers makes the first move. All men are moved forward diagonally one square at a time, to the right or left, onto vacant squares. A player captures an opponent's man by jumping over that man and landing on a vacant square just beyond. Two, three, or even more captures can be made during one move. If a man reaches the last row on the opposite side, it becomes a king. It is crowned by placing another man of the same color on top of it. A king can move only one vacant square at a time, but it can go either forward or backward. This gives it a great advantage. A king can go both forward and backward when making more than one capture during a move.

A player wins by capturing all of the opposing men or blocking them from moving. If neither player can win, the game ends in a draw. As a rule, players exchange colors after each game.

Checkers has many variations. In Spanish checkers, or pool checkers, an uncrowned man can jump backward or forward. In Turkish checkers, each player uses 16 checkers and can move them straight ahead or to either side, but not backward.

Team matches are popular. Today players compete in world, North American, and United States tournaments, each with its individual championship.

Reading Time _____

Recalling Facts

1. In Great Britain, checkers is called
   - ❏ a. draughts.
   - ❏ b. darts.
   - ❏ c. chess.

2. An American checkers player starts with
   - ❏ a. 8 pieces.
   - ❏ b. 10 pieces.
   - ❏ c. 12 pieces.

3. A player captures an opponent's man by
   - ❏ a. rolling dice.
   - ❏ b. jumping over that man and landing on a vacant square.
   - ❏ c. landing on the same square as that man.

4. A king has the advantage of
   - ❏ a. moving more than one square at a time.
   - ❏ b. moving either forward or backward.
   - ❏ c. jumping sideways.

5. A player wins by capturing all the opposing men or
   - ❏ a. blocking them from moving.
   - ❏ b. reaching the last row on the opposite side.
   - ❏ c. capturing the most men during a single move.

Understanding Ideas

6. A winning checkers player is most likely
   - ❏ a. uncertain.
   - ❏ b. daring.
   - ❏ c. predictable.

7. You can conclude from the article that the modern version of checkers
   - ❏ a. has ancient origins.
   - ❏ b. was invented in the nineteenth century.
   - ❏ c. was played by China.

8. A good checkers player might also be a good
   - ❏ a. golfer.
   - ❏ b. chess player.
   - ❏ c. tennis player.

9. You can conclude from the article that checkers is played
   - ❏ a. mainly in the United States and Great Britain.
   - ❏ b. mainly in Europe.
   - ❏ c. around the world.

10. Checkers is a game that requires
    - ❏ a. physical strength.
    - ❏ b. shrewdness.
    - ❏ c. a high I.Q.

Once a man carved a beautiful wooden checkerboard for his son. The boy took the board everywhere. One day he met some camel drivers. They were making a fire. "Where in this desert country of yours can someone get wood?" one driver asked the boy.

"Here is some wood," said the boy. He showed the man his checkerboard. The man put the board into the fire. As the board went up in flames, the boy cried, "Now where is my checkerboard?" So the camel driver gave him an ax in place of the board.

The boy took the ax and went on. He met a woodcutter. "My ax is too small. Lend me yours," the man said. But after a few blows, the ax broke. "Now where is my ax?" the boy cried. So the woodcutter gave him a log in place of the ax.

The boy took the log and went on. In the village, he met a woman who said, "Where did you find the wood? I need it for my fire." The boy gave the log to her. As it went up in flames, he cried, "Now where is my wood?" The woman gave him a fine checkerboard in place of the log.

The boy took the checkerboard and went home. As he entered his house, his father smiled and said, "What is better than a checkerboard to keep a boy out of trouble?"

1. Recognizing Words in Context

Find the word *fine* in the passage. One definition below is a *synonym* for that word; it means the same or almost the same thing. One definition is an *antonym;* it has the opposite or nearly opposite meaning. The other has a completely different meaning. Label the definitions S for *synonym,* A for *antonym,* and D for *different.*

_____ a. excellent

_____ b. worthless

_____ c. thin

2. Distinguishing Fact from Opinion

Two of the statements below present *facts,* which can be proved correct. The other statement is an *opinion,* which expresses someone's thoughts or beliefs. Label the statements F for *fact* and O for *opinion.*

_____ a. The camel driver gave the boy an ax in place of his checkerboard.

_____ b. There is nothing better than a checkerboard to keep a boy out of trouble.

_____ c. The woodcutter broke the boy's ax.

3. Keeping Events in Order

Label the statements below 1, 2, and 3 to show the order in which the events happened.

_____ a. The woman gave the boy a checkerboard.

_____ b. The woodcutter gave the boy a log.

_____ c. The camel driver burned up the boy's checkerboard.

4. Making Correct Inferences

Two of the statements below are correct *inferences*, or reasonable guesses. They are based on information in the passage. The other statement is an incorrect, or faulty, inference. Label the statements C for *correct* inference and F for *faulty* inference.

_____ a. The boy learned a lesson from his experiences.

_____ b. The boy did not expect the camel driver to burn his checkerboard.

_____ c. The boy's father thought the checkerboard was the one he had carved for his son.

5. Understanding Main Ideas

One of the statements below expresses the main idea of the passage. One statement is too general, or too broad. The other explains only part of the passage; it is too narrow. Label the statements M for *main idea*, B for *too broad*, and N for *too narrow*.

_____ a. A boy loses a checkerboard but gets one back after a series of exchanges.

_____ b. Once a man carved a beautiful checkerboard for his son.

_____ c. Checkers is a board game of ancient origin.

Correct Answers, Part A _____

Correct Answers, Part B _____

Total Correct Answers _____

The Florida Keys

The small islands off the coast of Florida are called keys. From Spanish, the word *key* means "rock" or "islet." The name *Florida Keys* refers to the chain of about 60 keys that extends from Miami Beach to Key West.

The eastern end of the chain is a remnant of an old coral reef. Living corals are still building reefs in the area. The western keys are made of limestone. Mangrove thickets line the shores and cover some of the low islands. The growth that rises on the higher ground is composed of tropical hardwoods and palms. Some small keys are submerged at high tide.

The largest of the keys is Key Largo. John Pennekamp Coral Reef State Park is located in the Atlantic waters off this key. Its chief attractions are underwater scenery and living coral formations. Settlements have sprung up on some of the larger keys. There is little agriculture because of the thin soil. Fishing resorts entertain people who come for deep-sea fishing.

The southernmost city in the United States, outside of Hawaii, is Key West. It spreads over a small island. It lies some 100 miles (160 kilometers) southwest of the mainland. The island is the westernmost in the Florida Keys. Its location provides sunny year-round warmth. Its shores are bathed by warm Gulf Stream water, and the southeast trade winds bring mild breezes.

Key West's history has been colorful. Spanish adventurers of the sixteenth century were early settlers. Pirate ships hid in the passes and waterways between the keys. The offshore reefs still hold the sunken wrecks of ships lost in sea battles of long ago.

The settlement on Key West became a city in 1828. Cuban cigar makers arrived and became successful. Sponge fishing was good. During the 1890s, Key West was Florida's largest city.

Since 1938, the Overseas Highway has linked Key West to Miami, 155 miles (249 kilometers) away. Many tourists use the highway to come to the island city. Hotels, motels, and other tourist facilities have been built. Today the tourist trade, the naval air station, and fishing provide the greatest employment. Shrimp are caught in the Gulf of Mexico. Giant sea crayfish are sold as lobsters. A cannery turns sea turtles into green turtle soup.

An aqueduct (pipeline for water) has been built by the federal government to supply badly needed fresh water to Key West and the other islands.

Reading Time _____

Recalling Facts

1. The Florida Keys include
   - ❏ a. 60 keys from Miami Beach to Key West.
   - ❏ b. 100 keys from Miami Beach to Cuba.
   - ❏ c. 50 keys from Ft. Lauderdale to Miami Beach.

2. The largest of the keys is
   - ❏ a. Key West.
   - ❏ b. Key Largo.
   - ❏ c. Miami Beach.

3. Settlers in Key West in the sixteenth century included the
   - ❏ a. Spanish.
   - ❏ b. Dutch.
   - ❏ c. Portuguese.

4. A current problem in the Florida Keys is
   - ❏ a. lack of salt water.
   - ❏ b. a food shortage.
   - ❏ c. lack of fresh water.

5. A major industry in Key West is
   - ❏ a. tourism.
   - ❏ b. hunting.
   - ❏ c. airplane construction.

Understanding Ideas

6. You can conclude from the article that a major tourist attraction in the Florida Keys is
   - ❏ a. a colorful past.
   - ❏ b. good weather.
   - ❏ c. Cuban cigars.

7. You can conclude from the article that the smallest keys are
   - ❏ a. the most crowded.
   - ❏ b. uninhabited.
   - ❏ c. wildlife sanctuaries.

8. It is likely that most of the food in the Florida Keys is
   - ❏ a. imported.
   - ❏ b. grown in greenhouses.
   - ❏ c. exported.

9. The water problem in the keys is most likely due to
   - ❏ a. industrial pollution.
   - ❏ b. an overabundance of salt water.
   - ❏ c. their distance from the mainland.

10. Without the tourist trade, the economy of the keys would probably rely mainly on
    - ❏ a. government funding.
    - ❏ b. construction.
    - ❏ c. commercial fishing.

A Dream Destroyed

Henry Flagler had a dream. His dream was to build a railroad from Miami, Florida, all the way to the southernmost point of the United States—the island of Key West. Some people said this could never be done. The Florida Keys are a chain of many small islands. To support the railroad tracks, bridges would have to be built over 128 miles (240 kilometers) of ocean. Only low coral reefs and limestone keys would provide anchor points for the bridges.

Construction began in 1905. For seven years, the tracks inched their way down the keys to Key West. This engineering feat was accomplished with swarms of vessels, dredges, seagoing cranes, pile drivers, floating cement mixers, and hundreds of workers. Hurricanes in 1906 and 1909 delayed but did not end Flagler's dream. The Florida East Coast Railway was completed in 1912. Just one year later, Henry Flagler died.

Flagler did not live to see his dream destroyed. In 1935, a monster hurricane roared across the keys with 18-foot (5-meter) waves and 200 mile-per-hour (322-kilometer-per-hour) winds. More than 800 people were killed by the hurricane. The killer storm's winds almost literally swept away the railroad. The trains never ran to Key West again.

1. **Recognizing Words in Context**

   Find the word *swept* in the passage. One definition below is a *synonym* for that word; it means the same or almost the same thing. One definition is an *antonym*; it has the opposite or nearly opposite meaning. The other has a completely different meaning. Label the definitions S for *synonym*, A for *antonym*, and D for *different*.

   _____ a. brushed

   _____ b. built

   _____ c. cleared

2. **Distinguishing Fact from Opinion**

   Two of the statements below present *facts*, which can be proved correct. The other statement is an *opinion*, which expresses someone's thoughts or beliefs. Label the statements F for *fact* and O for *opinion*.

   _____ a. Work on the railroad to Key West began in 1905.

   _____ b. Building a railroad across the Florida Keys was an impossible task.

   _____ c. The Florida East Coast Railway was completed in 1912.

3. Keeping Events in Order

Label the statements below 1, 2, and 3 to show the order in which the events happened.

_____ a. The tracks inched their way down the keys for seven years.

_____ b. A hurricane destroyed the railway.

_____ c. Henry Flagler wanted to build a railway from Miami to Key West.

4. Making Correct Inferences

Two of the statements below are correct *inferences,* or reasonable guesses. They are based on information in the passage. The other statement is an incorrect, or faulty, inference. Label the statements C for *correct* inference and F for *faulty* inference.

_____ a. Hurricanes are common in Florida.

_____ b. Because of storms, the Florida Keys cannot be connected by bridges.

_____ c. Henry Flagler believed that a railroad connecting the keys to Miami was important.

5. Understanding Main Ideas

One of the statements below expresses the main idea of the passage. One statement is too general, or too broad. The other explains only part of the passage; it is too narrow. Label the statements M for *main idea,* B for *too broad,* and N for *too narrow.*

_____ a. In 1935, a killer hurricane struck the Florida Keys.

_____ b. Henry Flagler constructed a railroad from Miami to Key West, which was completed in 1912 and destroyed by a hurricane in 1935.

_____ c. The Florida Keys are a chain of about 60 islands extending from Miami to Key West.

Correct Answers, Part A _____

Correct Answers, Part B _____

Total Correct Answers _____

The Need for Clean Water

People have come to realize how important water is. All animals and plants are mostly water. A person's body is about 65 percent water. People need to drink at least five pints (2.4 liters) of water each day. Big animals need about 15 gallons (57 liters) of water a day.

Water has other uses, too. It is used for washing and air conditioning. It is used for household work and gardening. Steel, gasoline, paper, and most other products are made with the help of water. Power plants use water for cooling. Farms, of course, need water to grow food.

Water is even used to carry goods and people around the world. Water is used for swimming, boating, and other kinds of recreation. Water is the home of many animals and plants, such as fish, whales, clams, and seaweeds. It is easy to see that life would be impossible without water. That is why it is so important to keep Earth's water clean and usable. Yet, polluted water is becoming very common.

Water that has become polluted is unsafe to use. Pollution can happen when sewage and other untreated wastes have been dumped into the water. Polluted water can smell, have garbage floating in it, and be unfit for swimming or boating. But even water that looks clean and smells good can be polluted. It may be filled with microorganisms and dangerous chemicals that cannot be seen.

People pollute water in a lot of ways. One way is to allow bathroom and factory wastes to flow through pipes and into waterways without being treated. Another way is to allow soil, fertilizers, and industrial wastes to wash from farms, building sites, and mining sites into waterways after a rain.

Bacteria can feed on some wastes. Other wastes can be diluted by water in waterways. But nature can only do so much. People are making more waste than nature can handle. More and better wastewater treatment is needed.

It is a fact that not all towns properly treat their drinking water. Many people think that the water they drink is safe. Most of the time it is. But about 4,000 Americans become sick each year from unsafe drinking water. Many more cases are not reported.

Clean water is so important to people's lives. They should make an effort to make sure they will always have enough of it for now and forever.

Reading Time _____

Recalling Facts

1. People should drink at least
   - ❏ a. one pint (about .5 liters) of water a day.
   - ➡❏ b. five pints (2.4 liters) of water a day.
   - ❏ c. ten pints (4.7 liters) of water a day.

2. A person's body is made up mostly of
   - ❏ a. bone.
   - ❏ b. skin.
   - ➡❏ c. water.

3. Without water, life would be
   - ❏ a. easier.
   - ❏ b. difficult.
   - ➡❏ c. impossible.

4. One cause of water pollution is
   - ➡❏ a. dumping sewage into waterways.
   - ❏ b. rain.
   - ❏ c. using water in air conditioning.

5. Thousands of Americans become sick each year from drinking
   - ❏ a. too little water.
   - ❏ b. too much water.
   - ➡❏ c. unsafe water.

Understanding Ideas

6. Water that looks and smells clean
   - ❏ a. is probably safe to drink.
   - ➡❏ b. may be polluted.
   - ❏ c. most likely contains dangerous chemicals.

7. The article suggests that water pollution is
   - ➡❏ a. a growing problem.
   - ❏ b. nothing to worry about.
   - ❏ c. a problem found mostly in farming areas.

8. The main cause of water pollution is
   - ➡❏ a. people.
   - ❏ b. animals.
   - ❏ c. nature.

9. The article suggests that water pollution
   - ❏ a. cannot be corrected.
   - ❏ b. can be corrected by nature.
   - ➡❏ c. can be corrected by people.

10. You can conclude from the article that the most effective way to end water pollution is to
   - ❏ a. treat drinking water.
   - ➡❏ b. treat wastewater.
   - ❏ c. ban swimming and boating.

24 B — Cleaning Up a Stream

Gary's science class was studying pollution. One day the class went on a field trip to survey conditions at a local river. The stream was a smelly mess, full of trash. "Phew!" Gary exclaimed. "We should do something about this!"

The next weekend Gary, some classmates, and their parents hiked along the river. They found a pipe from a local factory spilling foul-smelling fluid into the water. They made notes about where they found rusty shopping carts and old tires. A sign that said "No Dumping" had been knocked down. They made a note about that, too.

On Monday, Mariana called the state department of the environment to find out about local antipollution laws. Keisha called the department of public works to see about cleaning up the trash. Bruce wrote a letter to the factory owner, asking him to stop polluting. Gary wrote to the editor of the local paper.

Gary and his classmates found that cleaning up a polluted river is not easy. The government agencies worked slowly, but the class kept calling and writing to check their progress. The trash was hauled away. A new "No Dumping" sign appeared. Then they read in the paper that the factory owner had been fined for polluting and had agreed to stop. Everybody cheered.

1. Recognizing Words in Context

Find the word *cheered* in the passage. One definition below is a *synonym* for that word; it means the same or almost the same thing. One definition is an *antonym;* it has the opposite or nearly opposite meaning. The other has a completely different meaning. Label the definitions S for *synonym,* A for *antonym,* and D for *different.*

_____ a. made happy

_____ b. whispered

_____ c. shouted

2. Distinguishing Fact from Opinion

Two of the statements below present *facts,* which can be proved correct. The other statement is an *opinion,* which expresses someone's thoughts or beliefs. Label the statements F for *fact* and O for *opinion.*

_____ a. Keisha called the department of public works.

_____ b. The class found rusty shopping carts in the stream.

_____ c. People need to work to put an end to pollution.

3. Keeping Events in Order

Two of the statements below describe events that happened at the same time. The other statements describes an event that happened before or after those events. Label them S for *same time,* B for *before,* and A for *after.*

_____ a. Gary, some classmates, and their parents hiked along the river.

_____ b. Mariana called the state department of the environment to find out about local antipollution laws.

_____ c. They made notes about the conditions they found at the river.

4. Making Correct Inferences

Two of the statements below are correct *inferences,* or reasonable guesses. They are based on information in the passage. The other statement is an incorrect, or faulty, inference. Label the statements C for *correct* inference and F for *faulty* inference.

_____ a. Gary and his classmates worked effectively to get the river cleaned up.

_____ b. Legal action was required to get the factory owner to stop polluting the river.

_____ c. Government agencies are not really interested in local pollution problems.

5. Understanding Main Ideas

One of the statements below expresses the main idea of the passage. One statement is too general, or too broad. The other explains only part of the passage; it is too narrow. Label the statements M for *main idea,* B for *too broad,* and N for *too narrow.*

_____ a. Gary and his classmates successfully took on the project of cleaning up pollution in a local river.

_____ b. Gary and his classmates found that a local river was badly polluted.

_____ c. Water pollution is a serious problem for everyone.

Correct Answers, Part A _____

Correct Answers, Part B _____

Total Correct Answers _____

The Bobcat

The bobcat, also called the wildcat, is a relative of the lynxes. It resembles the Canada lynx but is smaller and lighter. It is usually about three feet (0.9 meter) long when fully grown and weighs around twenty-five pounds (11.3 kilograms). Its coat is pale tan with black spots on top and nearly white underneath. Its tail is very short. It looks as if it has been cut short, or bobbed, which accounts for the animal's name. The bobcat's hind legs are longer than its forelegs. This gives the animal an awkward, bounding gait when it runs. As with mountain lions, the number of bobcats has been greatly reduced. Because of this and because bobcats are secretive creatures, you are not likely to see them unless you search patiently.

If you see a bobcat before it sees you, it will probably be daytime. During the day, the animal may be sleeping under a thicket or under a ledge, digesting the meal it has caught the night before. Or you may glimpse one walking in the distance at twilight. As soon as the cat becomes aware of you, it will leap away. If you chase it, you may force it to climb a tree or dodge into a hole. There is little chance of running it down because it is an agile, clever, and sure-footed animal. It is a good swimmer as well and can escape by water.

The bobcat is a dangerous animal. There have been tales of bobcats attacking hikers, but none of the reports have been found to be true. Yet, a trapped bobcat can be unbelievably ferocious. People who have taken bobcat kittens for pets have often regretted it. They can become vicious on a moment's notice. Bobcats do not get along with house cats or dogs; they often attack pet cats and dogs on sight. They kill poultry, too, and, if hungry enough, sometimes attack lambs. This gives them a bad reputation, but the bobcat's normal diet consists of rabbits, rats, and other small animals. Its usefulness in controlling these pests far outweighs the damage it does. The number of rabbits killed by the average bobcat in its lifetime would be enough to destroy whole crops of vegetables.

Above all, the bobcat is versatile. It ranges among many types of habitats—forests, deserts, mountains, and plains. The tough and wily bobcat can survive in them all.

Reading Time _____

Recalling Facts

1. Bobcats are relatives of
   - ❏ a. wildcats.
   - ❏ b. panthers.
   - ❏ c. lynxes.

2. Bobcats get their name from
   - ❏ a. the awkward way they run.
   - ❏ b. their short tails.
   - ❏ c. their ability to float.

3. Bobcats are known to be
   - ❏ a. ferocious.
   - ❏ b. harmless.
   - ❏ c. poor swimmers.

4. The bobcat's normal diet consists of
   - ❏ a. small animals.
   - ❏ b. plants and insects.
   - ❏ c. cattle and lambs.

5. The bobcat's bad reputation comes from
   - ❏ a. false stories.
   - ❏ b. attacks on household pets.
   - ❏ c. its frightening appearance.

Understanding Ideas

6. The article suggests that the bobcat's bad reputation
   - ❏ a. is deserved.
   - ❏ b. should be maintained.
   - ❏ c. is not deserved.

7. The fact that their number is decreasing suggests that bobcats
   - ❏ a. could someday be in danger of extinction.
   - ❏ b. are being killed by mountain lions.
   - ❏ c. are becoming less adaptable.

8. It is likely that opinions about bobcats vary
   - ❏ a. from one part of the country to another.
   - ❏ b. from year to year.
   - ❏ c. according to a person's experience.

9. You can conclude from the article that bobcats are also called wildcats because of their
   - ❏ a. relationship to lynxes.
   - ❏ b. sudden viciousness.
   - ❏ c. attacks on hikers.

10. You can conclude from the article that the bobcat's survival is due mainly to
    - ❏ a. its ferocious nature.
    - ❏ b. its ability to adapt to its environment.
    - ❏ c. luck.

25 B   Night Hunter

As evening falls, a bobcat crouches at the edge of the woods, ears forward to catch every sound. Its green eyes dart about to pick up the slightest movement. Nearby, a cottontail rabbit is nibbling grass. The rabbit, too, is alert, but not alert enough to protect itself from one of North America's most efficient hunters.

The cat moves so silently that any sound it makes is no more than the whisper of the wind. As its eyes lock onto its prey, its short, stubby tail twitches slightly. The bobcat edges closer, gathers its muscles, and lunges out of the underbrush. Before the rabbit can flee, the cat stuns it with the swipe of a furry paw and quickly bites its neck. Grasping its limp prey in its mouth, the cat slinks silently back into the woods and disappears in the foliage, almost like a ghost.

Able to capture and eat a variety of prey and not highly valued for their fur, bobcats have remained more plentiful in number than other wild cats. But their habitat is shrinking steadily. No one knows how much longer these shy native cats will be able to range freely and hunt as they have always done.

1. **Recognizing Words in Context**

   Find the word *gathers* in the passage. One definition below is a *synonym* for that word; it means the same or almost the same thing. One definition is an *antonym*; it has the opposite or nearly opposite meaning. The other has a completely different meaning. Label the definitions S for *synonym*, A for *antonym*, and D for *different*.

   _____ a. tightens

   _____ b. loosens

   _____ c. picks

2. **Distinguishing Fact from Opinion**

   Two of the statements below present *facts*, which can be proved correct. The other statement is an *opinion*, which expresses someone's thoughts or beliefs. Label the statements F for *fact* and O for *opinion*.

   _____ a. A bobcat has a short, stubby tail.

   _____ b. We need to protect the environment in which bobcats live to assure their continued survival.

   _____ c. Bobcats eat a variety of prey.

3. Keeping Events in Order

Two of the statements below describe events that happened at the same time. The other statement describes an event that happened before or after those events. Label them S for *same time,* B for *before,* and A for *after.*

_____ a. The bobcat stuns the rabbit with a swipe of its paw.

_____ b. The bobcat grasps its prey in its mouth.

_____ c. The cat slinks silently back into the woods.

4. Making Correct Inferences

Two of the statements below are correct *inferences,* or reasonable guesses. They are based on information in the passage. The other statement is an incorrect, or faulty, inference. Label the statements C for *correct* inference and F for *faulty* inference.

_____ a. Bobcats are powerful hunters.

_____ b. Bobcats are threatened by civilization.

_____ c. Bobcats are a danger to humans.

5. Understanding Main Ideas

One of the statements below expresses the main idea of the passage. One statement is too general, or too broad. The other explains only part of the passage; it is too narrow. Label the statements M for *main idea,* B for *too broad,* and N for *too narrow.*

_____ a. A bobcat captures a rabbit by silently creeping up on it, knocking it down with a paw, and killing it with a bite.

_____ b. The bobcat, also called the wildcat, is a relative of the lynx.

_____ c. A rabbit, alert to danger, does not hear a bobcat until it is too late.

Correct Answers, Part A _____

Correct Answers, Part B _____

Total Correct Answers _____

ANSWER KEY

READING RATE GRAPH

COMPREHENSION SCORE GRAPH

COMPREHENSION SKILLS PROFILE GRAPH

ANSWER KEY

1A	1. a	2. b	3. a	4. c	5. c	6. b	7. b	8. c	9. b	10. b
1B	1. D, S, A		2. F, O, F		3. S, A, S		4. F, C, C		5. M, N, B	
2A	1. b	2. b	3. a	4. b	5. b	6. c	7. a	8. c	9. a	10. a
2B	1. A, S, D		2. F, F, O		3. 3, 2, 1		4. C, F, C		5. B, N, M	
3A	1. b	2. a	3. b	4. b	5. c	6. a	7. b	8. b	9. c	10. a
3B	1. D, S, A		2. O, F, F		3. 3, 1, 2		4. F, C, C		5. B, M, N	
4A	1. a	2. b	3. b	4. c	5. a	6. a	7. a	8. c	9. b	10. b
4B	1. S, A, D		2. F, O, F		3. 2, 3, 1		4. C, C, F		5. N, B, M	
5A	1. c	2. b	3. c	4. b	5. c	6. a	7. c	8. a	9. b	10. c
5B	1. D, S, A		2. F, O, F		3. 3, 2, 1		4. F, C, C		5. N, M, B	
6A	1. c	2. b	3. a	4. b	5. a	6. b	7. c	8. a	9. c	10. a
6B	1. A, D, S		2. F, O, F		3. 1, 3, 2		4. C, C, F		5. B, N, M	
7A	1. c	2. a	3. a	4. b	5. c	6. b	7. c	8. a	9. a	10. b
7B	1. S, D, A		2. F, F, O		3. 1, 2, 3		4. C, F, C		5. B, N, M	
8A	1. c	2. b	3. b	4. a	5. b	6. b	7. c	8. b	9. c	10. a
8B	1. A, S, D		2. F, F, O		3. 3, 2, 1		4. C, F, C		5. B, N, M	
9A	1. c	2. a	3. c	4. c	5. b	6. c	7. a	8. a	9. b	10. b
9B	1. D, A, S		2. F, O, F		3. S, A, S		4. F, C, C		5. B, N, M	
10A	1. b	2. a	3. a	4. b	5. c	6. a	7. b	8. b	9. c	10. a
10B	1. D, S, A		2. O, F, F		3. 3, 1, 2		4. C, F, C		5. M, B, N	
11A	1. b	2. c	3. b	4. b	5. c	6. a	7. c	8. a	9. a	10. c
11B	1. A, S, D		2. O, F, F		3. 1, 3, 2		4. F, C, C		5. M, N, B	
12A	1. b	2. b	3. c	4. b	5. c	6. a	7. b	8. a	9. c	10. a
12B	1. A, S, D		2. F, F, O		3. 2, 1, 3		4. C, C, F		5. B, N, M	
13A	1. b	2. c	3. a	4. c	5. a	6. c	7. b	8. b	9. c	10. a
13B	1. D, S, A		2. F, O, F		3. S, B, S		4. C, C, F		5. M, B, N	

14A	1. b	2. c	3. a	4. b	5. c	6. a	7. a	8. b	9. c	10. a
14B	1. S, D, A		2. F, O, F		3. B, S, S		4. C, F, C		5. N, B, M	
15A	1. b	2. c	3. b	4. b	5. a	6. a	7. b	8. c	9. b	10. a
15B	1. A, S, D		2. F, F, O		3. B, S, S		4. C, F, C		5. M, B, N	
16A	1. b	2. c	3. a	4. c	5. a	6. b	7. a	8. a	9. c	10. c
16B	1. A, D, S		2. O, F, F		3. 2, 1, 3		4. F, C, C		5. B, M, N	
17A	1. c	2. c	3. a	4. b	5. b	6. b	7. b	8. c	9. a	10. a
17B	1. S, A, D		2. F, F, O		3. S, B, S		4. C, F, C		5. B, M, N	
18A	1. b	2. c	3. b	4. c	5. b	6. a	7. b	8. c	9. a	10. a
18B	1. D, A, S		2. F, F, O		3. S, S, A		4. C, C, F		5. B, M, N	
19A	1. a	2. b	3. b	4. c	5. c	6. a	7. b	8. b	9. a	10. a
19B	1. S, D, A		2. F, O, F		3. B, S, S		4. C, F, C		5. M, N, B	
20A	1. b	2. a	3. b	4. c	5. a	6. c	7. c	8. a	9. b	10. a
20B	1. D, A, S		2. F, F, O		3. S, B, S		4. F, C, C		5. N, M, B	
21A	1. c	2. b	3. b	4. a	5. c	6. a	7. c	8. a	9. a	10. c
21B	1. A, D, S		2. F, O, F		3. 2, 1, 3		4. C, F, C		5. B, M, N	
22A	1. a	2. c	3. b	4. b	5. a	6. b	7. a	8. b	9. c	10. b
22B	1. S, A, D		2. F, O, F		3. 3, 2, 1		4. F, C, C		5. M, N, B	
23A	1. a	2. b	3. a	4. c	5. a	6. b	7. b	8. a	9. c	10. c
23B	1. D, A, S		2. F, O, F		3. 2, 3, 1		4. C, F, C		5. N, M, B	
24A	1. b	2. c	3. c	4. a	5. c	6. b	7. a	8. a	9. c	10. b
24B	1. D, A, S		2. F, F, O		3. S, A, S		4. C, C, F		5. M, N, B	
25A	1. c	2. b	3. a	4. a	5. b	6. c	7. a	8. c	9. b	10. b
25B	1. S, A, D		2. F, O, F		3. B, S, S		4. C, C, F		5. M, B, N	

READING RATE

Put an X on the line above each lesson number to show your reading time and words-per-minute rate for that unit.

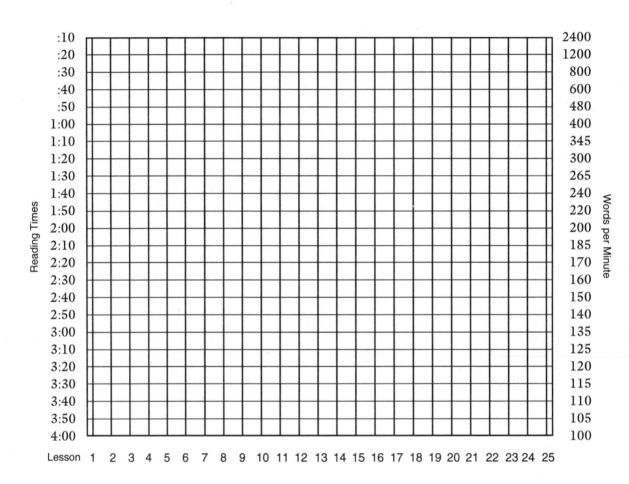

Reading Times		Words per Minute
:10		2400
:20		1200
:30		800
:40		600
:50		480
1:00		400
1:10		345
1:20		300
1:30		265
1:40		240
1:50		220
2:00		200
2:10		185
2:20		170
2:30		160
2:40		150
2:50		140
3:00		135
3:10		125
3:20		120
3:30		115
3:40		110
3:50		105
4:00		100

Lesson 1 2 3 4 5 6 7 8 9 10 11 12 13 14 15 16 17 18 19 20 21 22 23 24 25

COMPREHENSION SCORE

Put an X on the line above each lesson number to indicate your total correct answers and comprehension score for that unit.

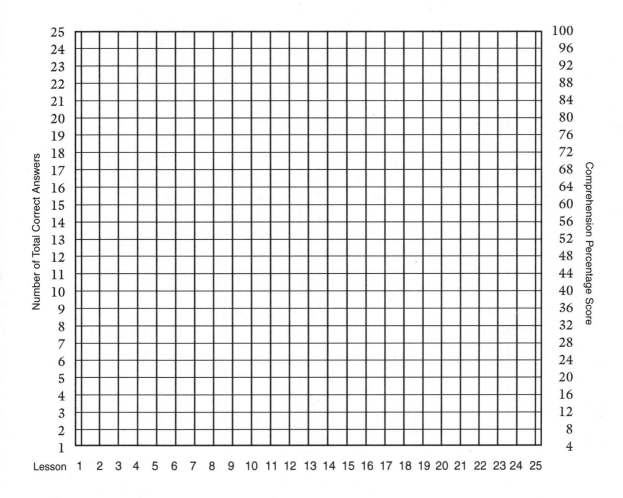

COMPREHENSION SKILLS PROFILE

Put an X in the box above each question type to indicate an incorrect reponse to any part of that question.

Lesson 1					
2					
3					
4					
5					
6					
7					
8					
9					
10					
11					
12					
13					
14					
15					
16					
17					
18					
19					
20					
21					
22					
23					
24					
25					

| Recognizing Words in Context | Distinguishing Fact from Opinion | Keeping Events in Order | Making Correct Inferences | Understanding Main Ideas |